DOLLY PARTON'S

JOLENE

Oxford KEYNOTES
Series Editor KEVIN BARTIG

Sergei Prokofiev's Alexander Nevsky
KEVIN BARTIG

Arvo Pärt's Tabula Rasa
KEVIN C. KARNES

Aaron Copland's Appalachian Spring
ANNEGRET FAUSER

Rodgers and Hammerstein's Carousel
TIM CARTER

Arlen and Harburg's Over the Rainbow
WALTER FRISCH

Beethoven's Symphony No. 9
ALEXANDER REHDING

Claude Debussy's Clair de Lune
GURMINDER KAUR BHOGAL

Brian Eno's Ambient 1: Music for Airports
JOHN T. LYSAKER

Alfred Schnittke's Concerto Grosso no. 1
PETER J. SCHMELZ

George Bizet's Carmen
NELLY FURMAN

Jean Sibelius's Violin Concerto
TINA K. RAMNARINE

Puccini's La Bohème
ALEXANDRA WILSON

Antonín Dvořák's New World Symphony
DOUGLAS W. SHADLE

Beethoven's String Quartet in C-sharp Minor, Op. 131
NANCY NOVEMBER

Gioachino Rossini's The Barber of Seville
HILARY PORISS

Laurie Anderson's Big Science
S. ALEXANDER REED

Shostakovich's Symphony No. 5
MARINA FROLOVA-WALKER & JONATHAN WALKER

Manuel de Falla's El amor brujo
CAROL A. HESS

Berlioz's Requiem
JENNIFER WALKER

Dolly Parton's Jolene
LYDIA R. HAMESSLEY

Oxford KEYNOTES

DOLLY PARTON'S *JOLENE*

LYDIA R. HAMESSLEY

Oxford University Press is a department of the University of Oxford. It furthers the University's objective of excellence in research, scholarship, and education by publishing worldwide. Oxford is a registered trade mark of Oxford University Press in the UK and in certain other countries.

Published in the United States of America by Oxford University Press
198 Madison Avenue, New York, NY 10016, United States of America.

Library of Congress Cataloging-in-Publication Data
Names: Hamessley, Lydia R., author.
Title: Dolly Parton's *Jolene* / Lydia R. Hamessley.
Description: New York : Oxford University Press, 2025. | Includes index. |
Identifiers: LCCN 2024058424 (print) | LCCN 2024058425 (ebook) |
ISBN 9780197760314 (paperback) | ISBN 9780197760307 (hardback) |
ISBN 9780197760338 (epub) | ISBN 9780197760321 | ISBN 9780197760345
Subjects: LCSH: Parton, Dolly. Jolene (Album) | Parton, Dolly—Criticism
and interpretation. | Country music—History and criticism.
Classification: LCC ML420.P28 H364 2025 (print) | LCC ML420.P28 (ebook) |
DDC 782.421642092—dc23/eng/20241216
LC record available at https://lccn.loc.gov/2024058424
LC ebook record available at https://lccn.loc.gov/2024058425

DOI: 10.1093/9780197760345.001.0001

Paperback printed by Integrated Books International, United States of America
Hardback printed by Bridgeport National Bindery, Inc., United States of America

Series Editor's INTRODUCTION

OXFORD KEYNOTES REIMAGINES THE canons of Western music for the twenty-first century. With each of its volumes dedicated to a single composition or album, the series provides an informed, critical, and provocative companion to music as artwork and experience. Books in the series explore how works of music have engaged listeners, performers, artists, and others through history and in the present. They illuminate the roles of musicians and musics in shaping Western cultures and societies, and they seek to spark discussion of ongoing transitions in contemporary musical landscapes. Each approaches its key work in a unique way, tailored to the distinct opportunities that the work presents. Targeted at performers, curious listeners, and advanced undergraduates, volumes in the series are written by expert and engaging voices in their fields and will therefore be of significant interest to scholars and critics as well.

In selecting titles for the series, Oxford Keynotes balances two ways of defining the canons of Western music: as lists of works that critics and scholars deem to have articulated key moments in the history of the art, and as lists of works that comprise the bulk of what consumers listen to, purchase, and perform today. Often, the two lists intersect, but the overlap is imperfect. While not neglecting the first, Oxford Keynotes gives considerable weight to the second. It confronts the musicological canon with the living repertoire of performance and recording in classical, popular, jazz, and other idioms. And it seeks to expand that living repertoire through the latest musicological research.

Kevin Bartig
Michigan State University

CONTENTS

ACKNOWLEDGMENTS

I am grateful to many colleagues and friends who offered support, guidance, and insights as I wrote this book. Kevin Bartig, series editor, was a generous reader and advisor during the project. I relished the opportunity he provided to continue my work on Dolly.

At Hamilton College, Alex Bádue, Victoria Betancourt Nieto, Heather Buchman, Jessica Burke, Ryan Carter, Gabe Condon, Adam Dudding, Ella Gant, Naomi Guttman, Rob Hopkins (emeritus), Nancy Rabinowitz (emeritus), Peter Rabinowitz (emeritus), Margie Thickstun, and Jane Springer read sections of the manuscript and offered valuable feedback. My students at Hamilton helped as well. Ryan Hayes shared valuable insights with me, and Carolyn Snowman assisted with the final manuscript preparation and the index. Haley Maddox, my student research assistant, read and critiqued the complete manuscript with a sharp editor's eye and helped construct the Comprehensive Playlist.

I am grateful for the support I received as the Eugene M. Tobin Distinguished Chair at Hamilton College. I thank

Ngoni Munemo, Vice President of Academic Affairs and Dean of Faculty at Hamilton College, for providing the platform to present my work as part of the "Conversations Across Disciplines" series and for supporting my travel to Dollywood. I also thank the reference librarians at Hamilton College, particularly Lynn Mayo and Kristin Strohmeyer, who tracked down several elusive sources for me, and Lisa McFall and Sara Mohr, who offered helpful guidance on constructing the companion website. Thanks also to Hamilton College Photographer and Digital Imagery Specialist Marianita Peaslee for providing some of the images in the book and to Graham Espe, Senior Multimedia Systems Technician, for recording some of the music examples.

Several people granted permissions for images and audio: Todd Alcott, Simon Attwell, Tom Berry, Tom Rutledge at Dolly Parton Enterprises, Leonard Taylor, and Ubiquity Records. Dolly's producer, Steve Buckingham, generously provided his studio chart for Dolly's recording of "Jolene" on *Something Special* (1995) as well as some insights about how he constructed the album.

I thank banjo player extraordinaire Cathy Fink, who advised on bluegrass influences, Jocelyn R. Neal, who offered guidance on musical theoretical matters, and Carol A. Hess for her good humor and wisdom throughout the process. Journalist Abbie Kozolchyk and I had a fruitful conversation about "Jolene" covers, the subject of an article that she was writing for the *Los Angeles Times*.[1]

I offer my deep thanks to the members of Chapel Hart—Danica Hart, Devynn Hart, and Trea Swindle—for the opportunity to spend time with them for an extensive interview. They were candid, thoughtful, and fun, and the behind-the-scenes look at their work was critical for my analysis of their music. Their manager Darrick Williams was also a great help.

Heather Buchman provided invaluable assistance with the musical transcriptions and analyses. Quim Rom Mas and his team at My Sheet Music Transcriptions worked diligently and patiently with me in preparing the musical examples.

Mary Volk, as always, was a keen editor throughout the project and an astute listener and critic as I worked out ideas through our many conversations.

Finally, I thank Dolly Parton for her generosity and songs.

ABOUT THE COMPANION WEBSITE

Oxford University Press has created a website to accompany Dolly Parton's *Jolene* that features a variety of related multimedia materials, including audio clips for all in-text musical examples. Many of these resources are integral to the volume itself or provide needed and useful context. As with all the websites for Oxford Keynotes volumes, the reader is encouraged to take advantage of this valuable online information to expand their experience beyond the print book in hand. Examples available online are indicated in the text with Oxford's symbol ▶.

www.oup.com/us/dollypartonsjolene

The reader is invited to explore the full catalog of Oxford Keynotes volumes on the series homepage.
www.oup.com/academic/content/series/o/oxford-keynotes-oks

RECORDINGS, MUSIC EXAMPLES, AND DOLLY

I HAVE COMPILED A COMPREHENSIVE Playlist of all the songs mentioned in the book, with a few exceptions. This playlist and other links to songs, videos, and recordings I discuss are available on the companion website for the book. However, within the text, I direct the reader to the companion website only for songs and videos that I discuss in depth. These examples are indicated with Oxford's symbol ⊙. At some points in the book, I provide time stamps of moments in the recordings I want to highlight for the reader.

The music examples I include are transcriptions of recordings rendered in notation to serve the analysis and are not intended to replicate every element in the example. The rhythms for the vocal parts are close approximations since Dolly and Olivia-Newton John sing in such an improvisatory, free style.

I refer to Dolly Parton throughout the book as Dolly, the persona she presents to the world (like Beyoncé, P!nk,

Drake, Enya, Adele, Rihanna, and Madonna). It is, after all, Dollywood, not Partonwood, and her first-name-only curly signature adorns her light pink stationery with a casual flourish.

INTRODUCTION

A JOLENE COLLECTION

IT IS EASY TO find items for a Dolly Parton Jolene collection fifty years after the 1974 release of her thirteenth studio album, *Jolene*. (Listen to example I.1 ▶.) There are Jolenes everywhere: uses of the song in films and television shows; noteworthy performances by Dolly; "Jolene" covers, answer songs, and remixes; images; performances of the song in Dolly's honor; AI versions; characters in plays, film, television, and books (who may or may not be named Jolene); the name of a country-rock band; a completely different song with the same title; and (perhaps) a real-life Jolene. Here are just a few notable examples from my Jolene collection:

- Beyoncé's cover/answer song to "Jolene" on her *Cowboy Carter* album (2024). (Listen to example I.2 ▶.)[1]

Dolly Parton's Jolene. Lydia R. Hamessley, Oxford University Press. © Oxford University Press 2025.
DOI: 10.1093/9780197760345.003.0001

- The song "Vaccine" sung to the melody of "Jolene" to promote the Covid-19 vaccine in 2020, written by Gretchen McCulloch and performed by Ryan Cordell.[2] Dolly sang her own version as she got her Moderna shot on video. (View example I.3 ▶.)
- The short film *Dolly's Song* by Kaylene Whiskey, an Indigenous Australian artist. Her painted images of Dolly and other pop culture figures and items sail by to a mashup soundtrack of "Jolene." (View example I.4 ▶.)
- A slowed-down version of Dolly's original recording of "Jolene" that went viral in 2013; the 45 rpm recording was digitally altered to 33⅓ rpm. Dolly's low voice is haunting, and the slow tempo reveals her vocal precision. (Listen to example I.5 ▶.)
- A Canadian nurse with red hair, green eyes, and fair skin named Juline Whelan. As a ten-year-old, Juline met Dolly and got her autograph in 1972, around the time Dolly wrote "Jolene."[3]
- Dolly's performance of the song with the a cappella group Pentatonix (2016). Their recording won a Grammy for the Best Country Duo/Group Performance, the only Grammy Dolly has received for "Jolene." (View and listen to examples I.6a and I.6b ▶.)
- A pre-revolution performance by Iranian singer Leila Forouhar. (View and listen to examples I.7a and I.7b ▶.)
- A red-headed, green-eyed woman named Polly is suspected of sleeping with another woman's husband in the neo-Western television show *Ride* (Hallmark Channel, 2023) in episode six, "Your Cheatin' Heart."
- The 2001 film *Women Talking Dirty*, the story of two friends. One sleeps with the other's boyfriend without

knowing of her friend's involvement with him. After his cheating ways are revealed, the two women become even closer. "Jolene" comments ironically on the events of the film when played during the closing credits.

- Dolly's legendary performance of the song at Glastonbury Music Festival (2014) to a crowd of about 180,000. (View example I.8 ▶.)
- Singer songwriter Bronwen Lewis's Welsh-language cover. (View example I.9 ▶.)
- The name of a vinyl wallpaper pattern. The maker writes, "Tired of the same ol' same ol'? Then it's time to explore the B-side!"[4]
- A mashup of a pulp novel cover illustration (figure I.1). Notice the "imprint" and "price" in the upper right. Dolly is from Pigeon Forge, and the album *Jolene* was released in February 1974 (2,'74).

These Jolenes rely on their audience's familiarity with Dolly's iconic cheating song. Simultaneously jaunty and haunting, the song's opening syncopated guitar riff and fast pace promise a fun ride while the unrelenting minor-key chord progression sounds troubled and obsessive. The chorus, with those four rising "Jolenes" in a row, invites audiences to sing along. But its lines quickly turn into pleading, and the melody falls back on itself. These repetitive elements combine to make the song feel predictable and stable. Yet the lyrics give listeners little certainty, particularly in the verses. In a surprising opening salvo to the "other woman," the first verse extols Jolene's beauty. The following verses raise more questions. As Annie Zaleski writes, "In the final verse, Parton sings, '*I had to have this talk with*

FIGURE I.1 Todd Alcott, Dolly Parton "Jolene" Pulp Novel Mashup Art Print. Courtesy of Todd Alcott Graphics.

you / My happiness depends on you,' but leaves it open to interpretation what kind of conversation this was—Polite? Threatening? Kind but firm? The continuation of that thought—'*And whatever you decide to do, Jolene . . .*'—doesn't illuminate much, as it too can be read as breezy, a stern warning shot or downright passive-aggressive. Whether the suspected affair was consummated or averted is also in question, which adds further mystery."[5] The song raises the prospect of infidelity without fleshing much out, aside from the physical description of Jolene.

My diverse collection of Jolenes is possible for several reasons. First, Dolly is an icon, and "Jolene" is one of her most well-known and compelling songs. When people allude to Jolene, they also evoke Dolly and all that she signifies. Second, the song is easily singable: "Jolene, Jolene, Jolene, Jolene." Third, the name Jolene is unusual and thus works well for the archetype of the "other woman." Fourth, the name and character are paired with a specific look (red hair, green eyes, ivory skin). Fifth, the song taps into the feeling of loss through a classic trope, the cheating song. For all these reasons, the song—and everything that comes with it (Dolly, the melody, the name, the image of Jolene, the story)—has become a cultural phenomenon.

The "distracted boyfriend" meme is a case in point (figure I.2). This photo had been circulating widely online since 2015. With Dolly's added captions, her song and its story attached immediately, and it went viral in 2018. Like this meme, several items in my Jolene collection are funny, silly, and lighthearted. But roiling underneath the humor is a serious story about the fear of loss.

Dolly Parton
@DollyParton

5:03 PM · 8/20/18 From Earth

121K Reposts **6.8K** Quotes

445K Likes **1K** Bookmarks

FIGURE I.2 Jolene meme (2018), original photograph by Antonio Guillem (2015).

NOT JUST A CHEATING SONG

The cheating song is ubiquitous in country music and goes back centuries to its roots. "Jolene" is usually at or near the top of cheating song lists. On the Taste of Country website in 2023,[6] it came in second to Hank Williams's touchstone country cheating song, "Your Cheating Heart" (1952).

However, "Jolene" is more than the cheating song label suggests. On the surface, Dolly's song is about a romantic triangle and possible infidelity. But there are multiple ways to read "Jolene." Hundreds of musicians, artists, writers, filmmakers, and listeners have used "Jolene" to express their own stories, viewpoints, and identities.

One of the most surprising uses of the song was revealed in the podcast *Dolly Parton's America* (Listen to example I.10 ▶) In the episode on "Jolene," listeners learned that when Nelson Mandela was imprisoned on Robben Island, he was allowed to select music to play over the prison PA system. He chose "Jolene." Tokyo Sexwale, one of the men imprisoned there at the time, described the significance of the song for Mandela and those who heard it: "We are all human beings: the jailed and the jailer. But we all come from one country. But we all don't want to lose. Whether it's a man, or your country, nobody wants to get hurt. 'Don't hurt me.'" Podcast host Shima Oliaee explained, "This song is not about love. . . . It's about fear, of someone taking your man, of losing everything. The prisoners feel that because they've lost their freedom. And the guards feel that because their country's changing, and they can sense they're about to lose power. Both are feeling the same fear, but for very different reasons."[7]

My study of "Jolene" takes several paths. In Part I, I do a deep dive into the song: its place on the album *Jolene* and how the album's other songs inflect the Jolene story; various ways to read the lyrics; and a detailed musical analysis. In Part II, I explore notable covers of the song: Olivia Newton-John's 1976 recording and several others that expand our perceptions of Jolene. Part III focuses on answer songs that respond to the song's ambiguity about Jolene's ultimate decision. I give special attention to Chapel Hart's sassy answer: "you can have him Jolene!" In Part IV, I return to Dolly and to Jolene, surveying how Dolly has reimagined the song in new ways and re-examining the "Jolene" origin story from a new perspective.

All these approaches to "Jolene" are possible because the song is, in a sense, unfinished. As Zaleski writes, "Jolene" is "so appealing because it's open-ended. . . . While we know how upset the song's protagonist is, we're not quite sure how her story ends."[8] I believe the song's ambiguity is at the root of its power. What is not ambiguous, however, is the fear of possible loss. Not just the loss of a partner, but the loss of something bigger and more abstract and ineffable. I also hear something else in the song: yearning. One can yearn for something they have lost. But one can also yearn for something they have never had and may never have—which is a kind of meta loss.

While writing this book, there have been times I have wondered if a little two-and-a-half-minute song merited all this attention. I was always certain of the song's excellence and craft; it is Dolly at her best as a songwriter. But as I engaged with the many ways people have responded to the song, I was also convinced that "Jolene" is worthy of our reflection and study because it has so much meaning, and means so many different things, for so many different people.

PART I

"JOLENE"

CHAPTER 1

JOLENE, *THE ALBUM*

DOLLY DROPPED A DELICIOUS tidbit for her fans in 2017—that she wrote "Jolene" and "I Will Always Love You" on the same day. At least that was the viral takeaway from her interview on *The Bobby Bones Show*. What she actually said was more nuanced and accounted for some lapses in memory:

BOBBY BONES: "You wrote ["I Will Always Love You"] how long ago?"

DOLLY: "In 1972, I think I wrote it—at the same time I wrote 'Jolene.' That was a good writing day."

BOBBY BONES: "You wrote it in the same day?"

DOLLY: "Yeah, I believe so. It was right in that writing period of time, 'cause I remember all my paperwork, and

Dolly Parton's Jolene. Lydia R. Hamessley, Oxford University Press. © Oxford University Press 2025.
DOI: 10.1093/9780197760345.003.0002

> like they came out pretty close, you know, at the same time. So, everybody said, 'boy, what was you taking? That was a good writing day.' But it was."[1]

In a 2004 interview, she had told a more specific story:

> I remember sittin' down in the corner of this couch, and I wrote ["I Will Always Love You"] in a couple of hours. . . . And while I was at it, I wrote "Jolene." A lot of people don't know that I wrote those two songs the same night, the same writing session.[2]

But in 2020, when asked about writing the songs on the same day, she said:

> Well, I'm not certain. But I tell you this. We found an old cassette when we were getting through all my songs, going down in my basement and all those old cassettes where I had written songs, and "Jolene" and "I Will Always Love You" was on the same cassette. So, if I didn't write it on the same day, it was during that same week or that period of time while I still had that particular cassette in my little player at the time. So, it's very possible.[3]

Did she write the songs on the same day, the same night? During the same writing session or the same week? No matter. These accounts reveal that Dolly was on a roll. She is a prolific songwriter, jotting down ideas whenever they come to her—when she is on her tour bus or cooking or even in the bathtub. Dolly was especially productive during the late 1960s through the 1970s. To borrow an apt phrase from Mayer Nissim, this was Dolly's "imperial phase."[4] From 1971 to 1975, she released two albums a year

FIGURE 1.1 "Jolene" and "I Will Always Love You" highlighted on the cover of Dolly Parton's album *Jolene* (1974).

and wrote hundreds of songs, many that are classics. So it is no wonder that the precise dates of her songwriting are a bit fuzzy. Nonetheless, it is remarkable that within a very short period Dolly wrote two of her most acclaimed songs. That they ended up on the same album just gilds the lily.

THE ALBUM

Jolene was Dolly's thirteenth studio album ▶. According to country music critic and historian Robert Oermann,

Jolene articulated a major shift in her career, both in style and in Dolly's stature as an artist. *Bubbling Over* (1973), released five months before *Jolene*, "could be considered her last 'starlet' album. Beginning with *Jolene*, her next solo LP, Parton was indisputably a major country star. . . . The title tune provided her with her first super-sized country solo hit."[5]

The album's cover highlighted not only the title song, but also "I Will Always Love You," the two most significant songs on the recording, which was released in February 1974 (figure 1.1) That was a pivotal year for Dolly. After a seven-year stint on *The Porter Wagoner Show*, she left to pursue a solo career. Dolly had joined the country music variety show as Porter's sidekick in 1967. She planned to stay for only five years, but Porter balked at letting her leave. Finally, two years later, Dolly made the break. She delivered the news to Porter through her song "I Will Always Love You." (Listen to example 1.1 ▶.) He got the message and said she could go if he produced the song.

During her last years with Porter, Dolly had her first #1 hit on the *Billboard* Country Chart in 1971 with "Joshua" (nominated for a Grammy), and that same year her album *Coat of Many Colors* charted at #7.[6] Four more albums followed, two in 1972 and two in 1973. And then, in 1974, her successes multiplied rapidly. She released two albums, *Jolene* and *Love Is Like a Butterfly*, and she scored four #1 hit singles: "Jolene" in February; "I Will Always Love You" in June; "Please Don't Stop Loving Me," a duet with Porter Wagoner, in October; and "Love Is Like a Butterfly" in November. "Jolene"—a 3X Platinum single—led off Side One of *Jolene*; "I Will Always Love You," Side Two. The album peaked at #6 on the Country Chart and is certified Gold. Dolly wrote all but two of the songs on the album. The music industry recognized Dolly's "triumphant" year, and she was featured on the cover of the issue of *Country Music* magazine that focused on women in country music (figure 1.2).

At the time of its release, critics recognized *Jolene*'s excellence. *Billboard* wrote, "With the title taken from her latest hit single, Dolly goes about recording a whole bunch of others—hits, that is. There are perhaps five or six here which could stand on their own."[7] Bob Adels, in *Country Music Beat* in 1974, commented about the many emotional facets of Dolly's voice as well as her songwriting talent showcased in the album:

> On the one hand is that spritely soprano twang of hers, unequalled on any scale you care to choose. Ever distinctive and dramatic, it is a voice that can convey the greeting card smiles of "River of Happiness," the tear-laden tenderness of "Lonely Comin' Down," and even the highly-stylized '50s-ish beltin' ballad pose of "I Will Always Love You"—the latter bringing back a sound we haven't heard since Brenda Lee's first few hits. Dolly's voice is always hers, but always the song's as well. And on the other hand are those very songs, most of which she writes herself. Her melodies reflect the purity of America's oldest folk song tradition; her lyrics are sometimes clean, ofttimes smudgy, windows of experience on which we've all pressed our nose at one time or another.[8]

In 2007, when *Jolene* was reissued along with her albums *Coat of Many Colors* (1971) and *My Tennessee Mountain Home* (1973), critics reflected on their place in Dolly's

FIGURE 1.2 Cover of *Country Music* magazine (July 1974) proclaiming "Dolly Triumphant!"

career. *No Depression* magazine called them Dolly's "first masterpieces. Recorded over roughly four years, they projected the full force of her magnificently pure vocals and brilliantly observational songs. Unlike the bulk of early 1970s Nashville fare, her work addressed complex subjects directly, yet with simplicity and nuance, her flair for stark, gothic Appalachian numbers comparable to ancient folk ballads."[9] Dave Heaton said these three recordings were Dolly's albums of independence:

> Taken next to *Coat of Many Colors* and *My Tennessee Mountain Home*, *Jolene* seems like a progression from those albums' theme that the modern world is a maddening, sad place. *Jolene* acknowledges that heartbreak—turned it into hit songs, even—but also pushes away from it, with an overall idealism. . . . Musically *Jolene* represents sophistication, maturation as well. It's the same instrumentation . . ., but the overall sound is smoother, slicker. . . . In *Jolene* it's easy to hear why Parton's leap of independence was ultimately also a cementing of her larger-than-life celebrity status.[10]

Not long after *Jolene*'s release in 1974, Dolly began her move to a pop crossover style. In an interview with Dolly's biographer Alanna Nash, Brenda Lee said, "I think Dolly's one of the best and truest folk writers and singers that we have." But, as Nash reported, Lee "agrees that after 'Jolene,' Dolly's music became increasingly harder to categorize." Nash elaborates: "by the fall of 1974, after the advent of 'Jolene,' she had managed to get Porter to allow her to put some lighter, pop sounds down on vinyl."[11] Nash is pointing to "Love Is Like a Butterfly," the title song of the album that followed *Jolene*. (Listen to example 1.2 ▶.) That song is as much pop as country (it went to #1 on the Country Chart but also appeared on the Adult Contemporary Chart at #38). Nash calls the song "whimsical" and says it fits "no category except, as its author would have it, 'Dolly Parton music.'"[12] For the next three years, Dolly's albums included more songs that leaned toward pop, and, in 1977, Dolly had her first major pop crossover hit, "Here You Come Again," written by Barry Mann and Cynthia Weil. (Listen to example 1.3 ▶.) As Dolly was making her crossover move, critics looked back nostalgically to the songs on *Jolene*, like "I Will Aways Love You" and "Jolene," as "simple, affecting country tunes."[13]

THE JOLENE SAGA

I think of *Jolene*, loosely, as a concept album, even though its songs are not connected as strongly as the notion of a concept album suggests. *Jolene* gives it listeners several options: you can revel in four songs celebrating happiness in romantic relationships—"Highlight of My Life," "Randy," "River of Happiness," "It Must Be You"—or wallow in heartbreak in four songs—"Jolene," "When Someone Wants to Leave," "Living on Memories of You," "Lonely Comin' Down." You might also enjoy a contemplative turn through two songs that transcend the happy/heartbreak polarity. "I Will Always Love You" is about an enduring love in a relationship (lovers, friends, parents) that is not going to continue in its present form. "Early Morning Breeze" is Dolly's meditation on her relationship with God through nature and is a welcome respite from the emotion-laden songs. But "Jolene" is the album's focal point, especially if, as Dolly's original listeners likely did, you drop the needle on "Jolene" at the beginning of Side One. With the song in mind, you can hear the group of happiness songs as the world that Jolene is breaking up, and you can hear the heartbreak group as the aftermath of Jolene's treachery. I think of the latter group as the Saga of Jolene.[14]

The 2007 reissue of *Jolene* included four additional songs written by Dolly that she recorded in the same sessions as the 1974 album ▶. Three of these songs strengthen the concept album reading: "Last Night's Lovin'" joins the songs about a happy relationship, while "Barbara on Your Mind" and "Another Woman's Man" expand the Jolene saga of heartbreak. (The fourth song, "Cracker Jack," is about a child's beloved dog.)

In "Barbara on Your Mind," a cheating man calls the name of the other woman in his sleep—"last night you said 'I love you' with Barbara on your mind." (Listen to example 1.4 ▶.)[15] The song includes the narrator's physical description of the lover ("I find traces of her kisses on your skin and strands of chestnut hair that say you've been with her again") as in "Jolene" ("your beauty is beyond compare with flaming locks of auburn hair"). In "Another Woman's Man," Dolly sings from the perspective of the "Jolene" character who is tempted by a man who already has a partner. But she does not have an affair: "I'd be lying if I told you I didn't want to love you, but I would never take another woman's man." (Listen to example 1.5 ▶.)

With the addition of these two songs, the Saga of Jolene comes into sharper focus. I imagine them laying out the story chronologically, with comments by the narrator:

"JOLENE": I'm afraid Jolene will take you. I'm going to talk to her about it.

"Barbara on Your Mind": I have evidence you're cheating on me.

"When Someone Wants to Leave": I need to let you go.

"Lonely Comin' Down": You've left me alone.

"Living on Memories of You": I think about you all the time.

"Another Woman's Man": I wish Jolene had made this decision; and I won't be a Jolene myself.

But there is another reading that addresses the song's ambiguity. "Jolene" and "Another Woman's Man" were recorded on the same day. I imagine the vibe that these two songs brought to the studio that day and see them as ripe for dramatization. They form a multilayered dialogue: the narrator talks to Jolene, who then talks to the man in the triangle, letting him know she will not take him from his partner.

"Jolene": I'm afraid Jolene will take you. I'm going to talk to her about it.

"Another Woman's Man": Jolene says she won't take you.

For all the ambiguity of the song (what does Jolene decide?), "Another Woman's Man" gives us a possible answer.

JOLENE BEFORE AND AFTER "JOLENE"

The cheating scenario is one that Dolly explored prior to and after she wrote "Jolene," and these other songs flesh out the "Jolene" saga. In "She Never Met a Man (She Didn't Like)" (*Coat of Many Colors*, 1971), Dolly pleads with her man not to leave her for the type of woman who, like Jolene, can take him "just because she can." (Listen to example 1.6 ▶.) The singer tries to make him understand that: "you mean no more to her than all the others she's held tight." The song points to the later "Jolene" in the way the narrator sizes up the scenario, doubts the other woman's sincere interest in her man, and tries to intervene by pointing out the truth of the situation to one of the people in the affair.

Two years after "Jolene," Dolly recorded "Hey, Lucky Lady" (*All I Can Do*, 1976), a song that seems like a continuation of the Jolene saga with Jolene as the lucky lady:

> Hey, lucky lady, lucky lady, you are now the lucky lady
> Are you happy with my baby, you know you're a lucky lady,
> you lucky lady

Dolly sets these lyrics, incongruously, to an upbeat, bouncy country melody with touches of rockabilly guitar and boogie-woogie patterns tossed in between lines. The playful setting continues with the driving, syncopated rhythm of her wordplay on "lucky lady." (Listen to example 1.7 ▶.)

Many years after writing these songs, Dolly recorded "Best Woman Wins" (*Eagle When She Flies*, 1991), a country pop duet with Lorrie Morgan singing the part of the "other woman." (Listen to example 1.8 ▶.) Here Dolly confronts another "Jolene" character, and neither woman will concede. Both will "fight 'til the end" and will "beg" and "plead." But despite their willingness to "suffer and bleed," they do not sound at odds with one another. Rather, they sing the chorus together in harmony and declare that their shared lover must pick the winner.

Some years later, in her country pop song "Cologne" (*Backwoods Barbie*, 2008), Dolly writes again from the perspective of the other woman. (Listen to example 1.9 ▶.) Here the "Jolene" character sings, "I'm not out to hurt someone, not you, not her, not anyone." To hide their affair, her lover asked that she not wear cologne because she's "a scent you can't take home." Knowing that he still loves his partner at home, the singer wonders, "will I ever get to wear cologne?"

Each of these songs takes on an added richness when heard in the context of "Jolene." Moreover, listening to "Jolene" in the company of these songs can influence and expand our reading of "Jolene." When we listen to "Jolene," we hear one story: a woman is afraid that another woman is going to take her man, and she begs her not to do it. Well, we *think* we hear one story. We can construct a whole scenario about Jolene as a homewrecker, but there is much we do not know about Jolene or her intentions. As the constellation of Dolly's Jolene songs grows—the other songs on the original and reissued album as well as related songs that precede the album and come later—the possibilities for the story multiply, and we see that Jolene may not be as straightforward as we initially thought.

CHAPTER 2

READING "JOLENE"

DOLLY TELLS THIS STORY about how she came to write "Jolene." After a show one night in the early 1970s, she was signing autographs. A little girl came up to meet Dolly and captured her attention. She had "beautiful red hair, this beautiful skin, these beautiful green eyes," Dolly recalled. She told the girl she was "the prettiest little thing I ever saw" and asked her name.[1] It was Jolene.

Dolly was charmed by the name and decided to use it in a song. On the way back to her dressing room, Dolly sang "Jolene, Jolene, Jolene, Jolene" over and over so she would remember the name. She was not sure at first what to write about. But, as she often does in her songwriting, Dolly went to her memory bank of experiences and recalled that she often kidded her husband Carl Dean about a flirtation he

Dolly Parton's Jolene. Lydia R. Hamessley, Oxford University Press. © Oxford University Press 2025.
DOI: 10.1093/9780197760345.003.0003

had with a bank teller. She explained: "He just loved going to the bank because she paid him so much attention. It was kinda like a running joke between us—when I was saying, 'Hell, you're spending a lot of time at the bank. I don't believe we've got that kind of money.'"[2] So Dolly transformed Jolene from a little girl into "the other woman." Years later, Dolly downplayed the cheating angle: "It is true that my husband got a crush on a girl at the bank. But that was not that big of a deal."[3]

By the time Dolly wrote "Jolene" in the early 1970s, Loretta Lynn had written and recorded two songs that set the tone at the time for cheating songs. Comparing "Jolene" with Lynn's songs reveals the complexity and ambiguity of Dolly's narrative: is the singer pleading or assertive, vulnerable or gutsy? I tackle this question by placing her lyrics in the context of Appalachian balladry and exploring the ways critics, listeners, and performers have read and interpreted "Jolene" through their own lenses.

A NEW APPROACH TO THE CHEATING SONG

Loretta Lynn was looking for a fight in her cheating songs. In "You Ain't Woman Enough (To Take My Man)" (1966), she threatens violence ("It'll be over my dead body, so get out while you can"). She does not feel inferior ("He took a second look at you, but he's in love with me"), and she insults her rival ("Women like you they're a dime a dozen, you can buy 'em anywhere"). Lynn's musical setting—classic country leaning to honky-tonk—reinforces the song's aggressiveness. In "Fist City" (1968), her lyrics are even more combative and are matched by the rockabilly energy that kicks off the song's threats of violence ("I'll grab you by the hair o' the head and I'll lift you off o' the ground"). Again, the singer verbally diminishes the other woman ("I'll show you what a real woman is since you think you're hot stuff"), and the insults fly ("But the man I love when he picks up trash he puts it in a garbage can").

While the betrayed woman in Lynn's songs is confident, Dolly's narrator is insecure ("I cannot compete with you"). Dolly believes this is what makes her song so popular: "everyone can relate to her feelings of inadequacy—competing with that tall redhead in the bank who was after her husband."[4] Although, like Lynn, the singer confronts the other woman, she does not threaten violence, nor does she insult Jolene. Instead, she sings about Jolene's beauty.

Dolly's approach in "Jolene" is classy. In the place of threats and insults, she simply, honestly takes her case right to Jolene. This attitude is reminiscent of Dolly's calm, taking-the-high-road responses in her infamous interview with Barbara Walters, who baited Dolly throughout their conversation ("you don't have to look like this," "would I have called you a hillbilly?" "do you give your measurements?"). Dolly never lost her cool: "We were very proud people. People with a lot of class. It was country class." With her eloquent answers, Dolly serenely rose above the insults. Walters was outclassed.[5] (View example 2.1 ▶.)

YOUR BEAUTY IS BEYOND COMPARE

A typical cheating scenario involves three people—"erotic triangles," in Eve Sedgwick's words. But cheating songs often focus on two people: the one who is betrayed and the one who is the rival for the "beloved" (husband/wife/

partner). In "Jolene," Dolly captures the emotional dynamics that form an intense bond between the betrayed and the rival, as "potent as the bond that links either of the rivals to the beloved."[6]

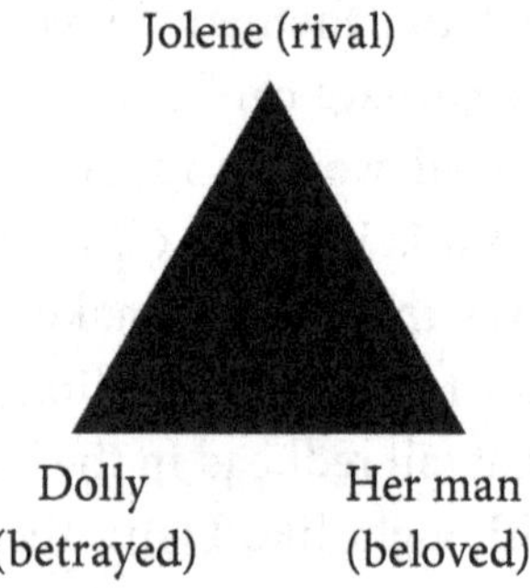

This bond is strongest in the first verse:

> Your beauty is beyond compare
> With flaming locks of auburn hair
> With ivory skin and eyes of emerald green
> Your smile is like a breath of spring
> Your voice is soft like summer rain

Dolly's biographer Alana Nash felt that it was only this "outstanding descriptive" verse that made an otherwise "not all that special" storyline compelling.[7] I disagree. These lines are not the only noteworthy element of "Jolene," though they are the most distinctive. Nonetheless, this verse is what most captivates and often puzzles listeners and critics.

When Dolly wrote this first verse, she experimented with different word choices, as visible in her hand-written lyrics (figure 2.1a). There on line 3, we see that Dolly's first instinct was the lyric as we know it: "with ivory skin and eyes of emerald green." It is evident from the different thickness of her pencil lines that she came back to that phrase and tried out other options, substituting "satin," "china," and "alabaster" for "ivory."[8] She also made the notation to herself that if she used "alabaster," she would have to omit the word "emerald" to make the poetry scan correctly (Dolly: "or just eyes of green if I use alabaster"). Compare these versions, saying or singing each in the song's rhythm:

> With ivory skin and eyes of emerald green
> With alabaster skin and eyes of green

Dolly chose the more elegant and most vivid line: "ivory" is a simpler and unambiguous way to describe fair skin. Keeping "*ivory*" also meant that she could retain "*emerald*," further filling the verse with layers of color as she did in the preceding line, "*flaming* locks of *auburn* hair."[9]

The way Dolly uses adjectives referring to color to describe a woman is reminiscent of lines from Appalachian ballads—like those Dolly heard growing up[10]—in which women have "long yellow hair," "milk white hands," and "red rosy cheeks." Dolly was not the only songwriter to draw on these tropes of balladry. One example is "With Body and Soul," written by Virginia Stauffer and recorded by Bill Monroe in 1967:

> Her beautiful hair was as pure as gold
> Her eyes were blue as the sea
> Her lips were the color of summer's red rose
> And she promised she would always love me

While this language is similar to "Jolene," there is an important distinction. The lines in "With Body and Soul"

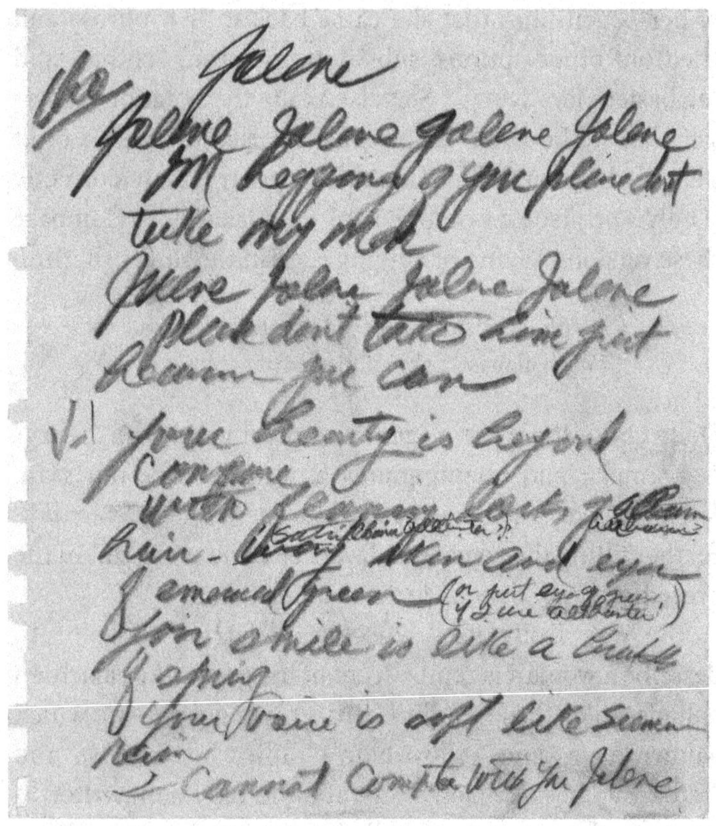
Jolene
Jolene Jolene Jolene Jolene
I'm begging of you please don't
take my man
Jolene Jolene Jolene Jolene
Please don't take him just
because you can
Your beauty is beyond
compare
with flaming locks of auburn
hair - ivory skin and eyes
of emerald green
Your smile is like a breath
of spring
Your voice is soft like summer
rain
I cannot compete with you Jolene

FIGURE 2.1a Dolly Parton, "Jolene," original lyrics. Courtesy of Dolly Parton Enterprises.

are sung by a man about his female love who has just died. Dolly's verse is intriguing because, in the original version recorded by Dolly, the lines are sung by a woman to another woman who is her romantic rival. This complicates matters.

Dolly's lyrics about Jolene's beauty prompt many questions. Does this rhapsodic language signal the singer's

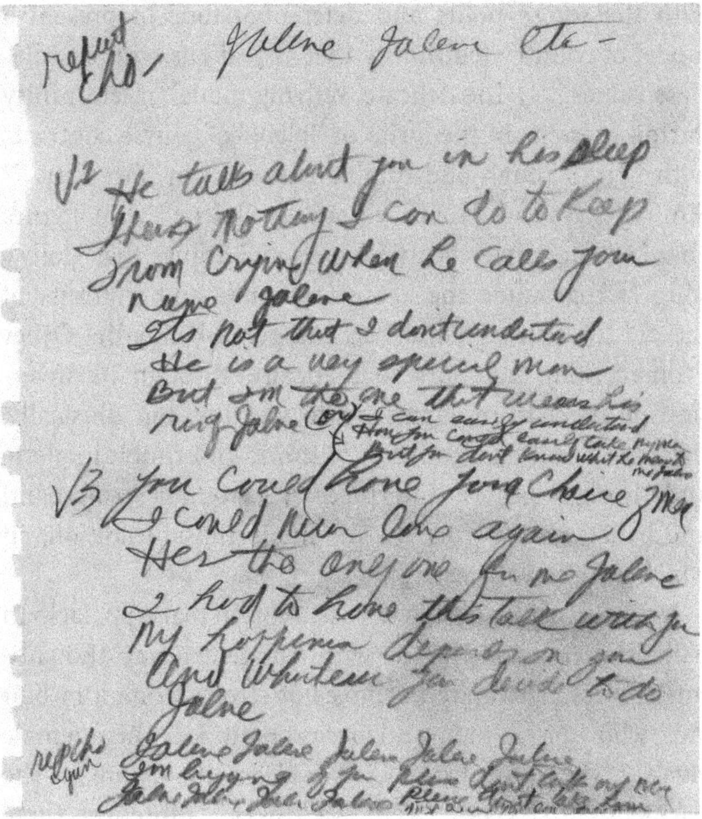

FIGURE 2.1b Dolly Parton, "Jolene," original lyrics. Courtesy of Dolly Parton Enterprises.

vulnerability? Does the singer admire or fear Jolene? Does the singer desire Jolene herself? Is the singer bold since she confronts Jolene so directly? Some musicologists look to Appalachian balladry and old-time music for answers.

Kate Heidemann argues that Dolly assumes a "submissive persona in 'Jolene'" and that the song's reliance on the archaic language of Appalachian balladry "combines with the song's polite and deferential tone to present a model of country femininity that also aligns with middle-class values. . . . The delicate, retiring model of femininity Parton presents in the lyrics of 'Jolene' of course contrasts with Lynn's rough-and-tumble character in 'Fist City.' "[11] Similarly, Nadine Hubbs compares "Jolene" with Lynn's "hard twang" style cheating songs and argues that Dolly's song "foregrounds the acoustic sounds and rhythms of the old-time string band . . . and genre-bends the Other Woman Song not only thematically, through its inversion of affect from aggressive to yielding, but musically, through its softening of the rhythmic and timbral palette and through generic intermixture invoking string-band and ballad norms from the mountain music traditions in which Parton was raised."[12]

It is fruitful to question the assumption that Appalachian balladry necessarily aligns with female delicacy and submissiveness. There are examples of strong women in ballads who outwit men and occasionally kill their female rivals ("The Elfin Knight," "Maid on the Shore," "The Farmer's Curst Wife," "The Twa Sisters"). Moreover, there are ballads about warrior women who enlist in military or naval service to follow their lovers into battle ("Willie Taylor," "Silk Merchant's Daughter," "Caroline and Her Young Sailor Bold," "Polly Oliver"). These examples challenge the conventional associations of balladry with only demure and retiring women.

VULNERABLE OR GUTSY?

Just as balladry embodies both vulnerable and strong women, these qualities can be true for the narrator in

"Jolene." Most critics read the song as a plea from a powerless woman. Porter Wagoner's biographer Steve Eng hears restraint in the singer's approach and suggests it is her yielding persona—"soft and tender" as opposed to Lynn's "angry, cutting" attitude—that "helped 'Jolene' reach a wider audience."[13] Similarly, Zaleski writes, "A major part of it is the narrator, who is an extremely sympathetic figure. The unnamed woman feels inadequate next to Jolene's beauty . . . and is despondent over her man's wandering eye. . . . [Dolly has] a desperate hint to her voice."[14] Another critic wrote: "Parton easily could have attacked this song with false bravado and insulted or threatened the temptress. Instead, she imbues the narrator with touching vulnerability and genuine concern for what she could lose, which seems more honest considering the situation at hand."[15]

These readings rely heavily on the rhapsodic lyrics of the first verse and on the pleading in the chorus. The singer also seems to abdicate her power through the reiteration of the word *you* throughout the chorus and verses of song. The word piles up even more in the final verse:

I had to have this talk with you
My happiness depends on you
And whatever you decide to do

This type of word repetition also links the song to the ballad tradition, which often includes refrains and incremental repetition of lyrics.

However, Dolly's deft use of repetition suggests something other than vulnerability and submission. Repetition is an effective rhetorical device (epizeuxis) used for emphasis and for heightening the listener's emotional response ("pay attention to me," even "I'm intimidating you"). The narrator's agency and rhetorical power are evident in her direct address to Jolene, even while Jolene seems to hold all the cards. This direct address is the strongest in each chorus, where Jolene is called out by name eight times. Yes, the singer could simply be pleading with Jolene. But there is something assertive about taking her complaint right to her rival (as Lynn does in her cheating songs). Rather than weeping alone about the situation, Dolly takes charge and confronts Jolene directly by name, leaving the other woman without a voice.[16]

Laura Cunningham, writing for *Cosmopolitan* in 1979, focused on the vulnerability in the song while suggesting a latent strength in singer:

> Hearing ["Jolene"], I recall the first time I ever listened to a Dolly Parton album. The occasion: a country-western songfest in the Los Angeles home of actress Susan Anspach. . . . Susan turned on a record player and said: "I want you all to hear this. This is *it*. The most vulnerable song ever written or sung by any woman. To sing this song, a woman must have no ego. *Listen*. . . ." *Vulnerable*. That's the word most often applied to Dolly. And, perhaps, an explanation of why women are so drawn to her: How can you resent someone who is so damned *vulnerable*? Standing in full regalia, she seems to be saying: *Go on, laugh at me, tell me I look ridiculous*. And so, by God, you can't.[17]

Vulnerable or gutsy? I hear both qualities in the song. It takes guts to be that vulnerable.

QUEER READINGS OF "JOLENE"

The vulnerability and gutsy-ness in the song are especially evident in the narrator's willingness to admire another woman's beauty so openly. Cunningham wrote that in Dolly's live performance of "Jolene," "she sounds oddly adoring, like a little girl to an admired big sister."[18] In the intervening years, critics have tended to read this adoration as erotic. One said that the first verse sounded like "a love ode by an Elizabethan poet to some reticent beauty."[19] Hubbs calls these lyrics "an ode to the other woman's beauty and desirability" and suggests a homoerotic reading of "Jolene." She writes, "I'm struck by the song's reversal of confrontational genre norms, its potent and moving transformation of female heterosexual rivalry into homoerotic reverie. . . . Am I the only listener who imagines her and Jolene getting together if the guy doesn't work out?"[20] When she was interviewed for the *Dolly Parton's America* podcast, Hubbs included a fourth verse that she wrote in which this scenario is played out.[21]

I am struck by the similarity between Dolly's rhapsodic lyrics and those by Sappho. Juxtaposing "Jolene" with Sappho's love lyrics to another woman demonstrates the extent to which Dolly's song allows multiple readings.

> He is a god in my eyes—
> the man who is allowed
> to sit beside you—he
>
> who listens intimately
> to the sweet murmur of
> your voice, the enticing

laughter that makes my own
heart beat fast.[22]

Sappho's lyric is a paean of desire by a woman who finds another woman enticing. As in "Jolene," Sappho describes the sonic beauty of another woman: the voice is a powerful site of her sensual power ("your voice is soft like summer rain"). Did Dolly write her lyrics with Sappho in mind? Of course not. When asked about this reading of the song, Dolly affirmed, "I guess if you were a lesbian you might think that, but I was not thinking that at all when I wrote it."[23] But if a listener is familiar with Sappho's poem or has a lived experience of being a woman desiring another woman, the homoerotic reading of Dolly's first verse is not far-fetched, but just one of the ways the lines can be understood. The bond between rivals in the song is so strong that, for some listeners, it can become the focus of the song.

"Jolene" is also a dynamic conduit Dolly uses to connect with her LGBTQ+ fans. Often in concert she will sing, "Drag queen, drag queen, drag queen, drag queen, I'm begging of you please don't take my man," usually followed by her comedic quip: "It's a good thing I was born a girl, otherwise I'd have been a drag queen."[24] Through her queer reading of that lyric, Dolly invites her LGBTQ+ fans to bring their own perspectives to the song.

"Jolene" has become a springboard for others to articulate further queer expressions. For instance, in the "I Kissed a Girl" episode of *Glee*, Coach Beiste sings "Jolene" as an inner monologue while watching another character, Sue, pursue the man she is interested in. (View and listen to examples 2.2a and 2.2b ▶.)[25] One twist is that Sue is only dating him to quell rumors that she is a lesbian. Another is that Coach Beiste embodies the "lesbian gym teacher" stereotype, even though her character is straight. Moreover, she sings "Jolene" just under an octave lower than Dolly, which further complicates the tangled sexuality issues of the situation.[26]

Another example is Amythyst Kiah's cover of "Jolene" performed with her band Her Chest of Glass. (View and listen to examples 2.3a and 2.3b ▶.) Kiah, a queer Black singer songwriter, has a powerful, deep voice that brings a sapphic resonance to her cover of "Jolene." Her 2014 performance of the song earned her a shout-out on the Country Queer website in a post celebrating lesbian country songs: "the listener [gets] the distinct sense that the narrator is actually yearning for Jolene herself."[27]

The Jolene/drag queen trope plays a pivotal role in the 2018 film *Dumplin'*, a coming-of-age story about a teenage girl, Willowdean, who idolizes Dolly.[28] Willowdean finds support and comfort in the local community of drag queens who sponsor Dolly-themed drag shows at a local bar. Her main advocate is Black drag queen Miss Rhea Ranged, who performs "Jolene" (she enters at 50:44). Netflix also promoted the film with a video of performers of *RuPaul's Drag Race* lip-syncing to "Jolene." (View example 2.4 ▶.)

WHO IS JOLENE, WHAT IS SHE?

We often look to origin stories for answers about the meaning of a song. So we return to Dolly's story about the red-headed bank teller. When she introduces "Jolene" in concerts or talks about the song in interviews, Dolly often includes this detail: "I fought that red-headed woman like a wildcat. She jerked my wig off and almost beat me to death with it. But I kept my husband. I got that sucker home, and I beat the tar out of him."[29] (View example 2.5 ▶.) Dolly tells this story to bridge the disconnect between the apparently weak woman in the song and the Iron Butterfly image that she projects. This anecdote embodies the vulnerable/gutsy dichotomy. When Dolly tells this hair-pulling story, she deftly balances two positions: she can perform the song as if she were the real-life victim of Jolene while simultaneously asserting her own power as the entertainer singing "Jolene." Dolly claims she gave as good as she got in their fight. Conceivably, some of Dolly's personal power transfers to the song's narrator.

Perhaps in adding the detail of the wig to her Jolene story, Dolly is also remembering another incident. Porter Wagoner recalls the following from their early days on the road together:

> I soon found out that she was actually an insecure person—in the way she looked, in the way she was brought up, in every direction. Believe it not, Dolly never used to think she was a beautiful woman, though of course she was. I feel sure that's a main reason she wears the big hairdos. One time she and the guys and I were horsing around on the bus, and I just accidentally knocked Dolly's wig off. Her hair was matted down real tight to her head, and she did look pretty bad. Well, I mean that just damned near killed her. It was a terrible, terrible thing; she cried about it. And of course I felt awful, because I didn't mean to knock her wig off. But I learned then how sensitive she was.[30]

Exposed in this way, Dolly felt humiliated, vulnerable, and insecure like the singer in "Jolene." Dolly wears lofty wigs and five-inch heels to appear taller than her five-foot frame. She included height when explaining why the song resonated with so many people: Jolene, the bank teller, "had everything I didn't, like legs—you know, she was about 6 feet tall. And had all that stuff that some little short, sawed-off honky like me don't have. So no matter how beautiful a woman might be, you're always threatened by certain . . . you're always threatened by other women, period."[31] It is hard to reconcile Dolly's description of inferiority in the song with its popularity among fans who joyfully sing along with Dolly: "Jolene, Jolene, Jolene, Jolene." But trying to resolve the ambiguities and tensions in the song should not be our goal.

"Jolene" is malleable, open to multiple readings, and the song's ambiguity is its strength. Having different interpretations adds to the song's appeal. As Zaleski writes, "Jolene" is "a choose-your-own-subtext song" and "musicians can put their own stamp on the bare-bones structure."[32] In the following chapter, we will examine the music of Dolly's song before turning to other artists' interpretations to discover what multiple readings and subtexts they bring to "Jolene" through their covers and answer songs.

CHAPTER 3

LISTENING TO "JOLENE"

Music critics and Dolly's biographers often describe "Jolene"—a karaoke and sing-along favorite—in ominous terms. In 1977, Jack Hurst called the song "chilling,"[1] and Jean Vallely commented, "'Jolene' has a haunting 'Ghost Riders in the Sky' flavor."[2] In 1978, Dolly's biographer Alanna Nash used similar language: "What made ["Jolene"] so eerily and chillingly effective, though, was Dolly's double-tracked harmony, so close and otherworldly as to raise goose bumps."[3] Soon after, a *Rolling Stone* critic spoke of the superiority of "Jolene": "In all of country music, there's nothing quite like the sense of accelerating dread that propels Parton's great 'Jolene.'"[4]

Dolly Parton's Jolene. Lydia R. Hamessley, Oxford University Press. © Oxford University Press 2025.
DOI: 10.1093/9780197760345.003.0004

ANCIENT RESONANCES

Writers frequently attribute these eerie qualities to the old-world, mountain music atmosphere in Dolly's songs. Hurst explained that Dolly's style, "more authentic folk than traditionally country," grew out of her exposure to the "musical heritage in the Smoky Mountain foothills."[5] In the previous chapter, we explored the influence that Appalachian ballads had on the lyrics of "Jolene." We will see in my musical analysis of "Jolene" that this influence goes beyond her lyrics. As Dolly said, "it was natural when I wrote to reflect back to the old songs we used to sing, and part of my melodies kind of carried that old-timey flavor without me realizing it until after they were done. And I still do that—those folky-type melodies are the best of all."[6]

The minor mode—specifically the Aeolian mode—of "Jolene" is what sounds spooky to these critics as well as to Dolly herself. She said that she loves minor chords and that they make the song "haunting" and "mysterious."[7] Some listeners, like Hurst, hear this modal sound as "folk-like," and Steve Eng describes the guitar lick intro of "Jolene" as "a folkie hammering-on, in a minor key."[8] But Eng also links this sonority to early English song: Jolene's "minor-chord melody has an antique 'Greensleeves' feel to it."[9] (Listen to example 3.1 ▶.) Nash makes a similar observation: "Beginning on a minor chord and progressing to only two more, both major, before returning home, 'Jolene' harks immediately back to the purest of Elizabethan form."[10] Many critics have commented that Dolly's music sounds Elizabethan, but there is nothing specifically Elizabethan about the chord progression Nash mentions.[11] The only link between "Jolene" and "Greensleeves" is the prominence of the modal ♭VII chord. However, rather than the English Renaissance, Dolly points to a source closer to home for this chord: "Well that's just that old mountain sound. It's the sorrow chord. . . . It's the feeling chord and emotional chord."[12]

Some scholars identify the minor mode of "Jolene" as Dorian.[13] Both Aeolian and Dorian are minor modes (with their lowered 3rd scale degree), and both have the ♭VII chord. However, the Dorian mode includes a raised 6th scale degree, which results in a major IV chord, a distinctive sonority that brightens the darker nature of the Aeolian mode.[14] To my ear, the faint and fleeting passing tones on the raised 6th in a few of the harmony vocals in "Jolene" are not structural nor strong enough to give the song the brighter quality of the Dorian mode. But these evanescent Dorian touches intensify the song's old-world atmosphere, as do the harmony vocals that are built on intervals of the 4th and 5th, which have a hollow, archaic sound as opposed to triadic harmonies. In describing the sound of the Dorian mode, Dolly said, "I like doing old-timey songs. It's in that minor key, which sounds old world to me, that lonesome drone."[15]

Internet Bardcore artist Hildegard von Blingin' likely found it easy to magnify the old-world sound of "Jolene" when she reimaged it as a medieval troubadour song (figure 3.1).[16] Her 2020 arrangement, more inspired by medievalism than by authentic medieval practice, included synthesized lutes, medieval-sounding bowed strings, and

FIGURE 3.1 Hildegard von Blingin', "Jolene" (2020).

percussion. (View and listen to examples 3.2a and 3.2b ▶.) Von Blingin' further amped up ye olde sound by including the raised 6th scale degree as often as possible, firmly placing her version in the Dorian mode that sounds, to Dolly, old world.

LISTENING TO "JOLENE"

How to begin analyzing the music of "Jolene"? It has a simple musical form. Yes, the song has just 200 words,[17] and the verse and chorus share the same chord progression. Its melody, harmony, and rhythm are repetitive. But I hesitate to use words like *simple* and *repetitive* to describe the musical elements of "Jolene" because they falsely suggest a lack of depth or craft. However, a close look at "Jolene" reveals the way Dolly shapes its elements for maximum impact. Her musical choices convey the song's anxious quality and ambiguity.

"Jolene" is in verse-chorus form:

Guitar Intro
Chorus
    Verse 1 "Your beauty . . ."
    Verse 2 "He talks . . ."
Chorus
    Verse 3 "You can have . . ."
Chorus
Coda

Like many popular songs in this form, it begins with the chorus to hook the audience. But the song has a second hook: the distinctive guitar intro.

GUITAR INTRO

Sometimes a song is instantly recognizable from the opening notes. This is true of "Jolene." We hear an acoustic finger-picked guitar riff playing a roiling, syncopated pattern that circles back on itself, returning again and again to punctuate ends of lines and sections. Like the lyrics of the song, it suggests multiple readings. Is it obsessive? Simmering with doubt? Nervous? Or is it assertive, relentless, and insistent? This earworm saturates "Jolene" with an energy that is thoroughly Dolly's: "I write the music into [my songs] like that little lick on Jolene, you know that's mine. You know I wrote that in it. I know very little music, but I make use of all that I know."[18] She said that after she wrote "Jolene" she "was excited about the little lick,"[19] which is "as much a part of the song almost as the song."[20]

Dolly "made use of" a lot in that four-beat pattern. But it is daunting to figure out exactly how she put the lick together—it is fast! I realized that listening to it hundreds of times was not going to be enough. So, I picked up my guitar. It was only by getting the lick in my own hands and fingers that I could understand its complexity. I never managed to get it up to tempo, but I got close enough to feel the tension between the right-hand picking pattern and the left-hand chords, hammer-ons, and pull-offs. Three different musical lines of the lick became clear, and the hypnotic swing of the riff was addictive. Once I got into that groove, it was hard to stop.

Dolly's recording of "Jolene" is in C♯ minor. To play in that key, a guitarist would capo the instrument at the fourth fret and play as if the song were in A minor. Thus, I will discuss the riff in A minor, since guitarists would think of the song in those terms. The riff is a four-beat pattern that occurs four times in the song's intro (example 3.1).[21] The implied harmony of the line is A minor, with a fleeting pass through G major on the fourth beat. Although accompanied by electric bass and percussion, the acoustic guitar alone comprises several lines of polyphony: a bass line, a backbeat, and a syncopated melody in the upper line. The interplay of these three lines creates an agitated, nervous energy that seems to rush ahead and then fall back in quick succession. (Listen to example 3.3 ▶.)[22]

The bass line of the lick is a drone: the pitch A sounds on every beat, even when the harmony of the melody shifts in beat 4 when the electric bass plays a G (or occasionally an E). This relentless acoustic guitar bass line helps create the obsessive quality of the song. The backbeat in the lick

EXAMPLE 3.1 Dolly Parton, "Jolene" (1974), guitar lick in notation and tab with three motives identified.

fills out the harmonic implications. The first two backbeats imply an A-minor chord (i or tonic chord) by sounding an E over the bass note A (on beat 2 the E is reached via a hammer-on from D). Beats 3 and 4 suggest a G-major chord (♭VII) through the D on the backbeat. (Listen to example 3.4 ⊙.) These two lines alone, of course, do not create the full chordal sonority, but they work in conjunction with the melodic line, which completes these implied harmonies. The steady bass and backbeat also provide a rock-solid grounding that makes possible the rhythmic complexity of syncopation, cross-rhythm, and polyrhythm that the melody introduces.

The melody line is only three brief motives that play an enlivened, syncopated rhythm. The first motive rises by step from A to B. Although, technically, the A is not sounded in the melody on beat 1, the ear fills in the A on the downbeat since the bass plays the A at that point. Also, right on that first beat, the guitarist sets the A-minor chord in position (minus the first finger), thus sounding a faint A via an unplucked hammer-on from the open G string to A. The sixteenth-note rest is the moment when the fingers contact the strings on the A chord. The following eighth note is the first plucked A that is played just after the downbeat.

The second motive vacillates between B and C in the same rhythm as motive 1. The initial note of this second motive is the first half of a quick hammer-on from B to C. The B occurs in the comparable space of the sixteenth-note rest of motive 1. The third motive has a pull-off from C to B with the same syncopated opening as the first two motives. But then it adds a note, dropping down to a quick G upbeat on the last sixteenth note in a syncopation that propels the melody back to the next downbeat. This melodic move to G, along with the D on the backbeat and the preceding B in the melody, solidifies the G-major chord (♭VII) and confirms the Aeolian mode for the song.

The syncopated rhythm of this melody gives the guitar lick its agitated, anxious feeling. But this atmosphere is created by something more complex than mere syncopation. When the three motives are played as a complete melody, they create an asymmetric cross-rhythm over the four beats in the bass. This means that the meter of the melody is not aligned with the four equal beats of the bass. Instead, the melody operates within an asymmetric meter of two longer beats followed by a shorter beat (two dotted quarter notes and one quarter note, as indicated in example 3.2). Both parts realign at the quarter note on beat 4 (just after the dashed bar line). (Listen to examples 3.5 and 3.6 ▶.)

This cross-rhythm is present in some bluegrass banjo licks (example 3.3). (Listen to examples 3.7a and 3.7b ▶.) Typically in bluegrass, over a four-beat measure, the banjo subdivides the beats and plays eight eighth-notes

EXAMPLE 3.2 Dolly Parton, "Jolene" (1974), guitar lick, three motives with primary cross-rhythm identified.

in patterns called rolls. In two of them, the forward and backward roll, the notes are not played in four groups of two (**1 2 1 2 1 2 1 2** or **1** & **2** & **3** & **4** &) but are played in an asymmetric pattern: **1 2 3 1 2 3 1 2**. Each number stands in for one of the eighth notes. To feel the rhythm, count the asymmetric pattern evenly with a slight accent on each **1**. Repeat the pattern in tempo with no pause. The faster you count, the easier it is to feel the asymmetry. You might even try clapping on each **1** as you speed up. This is the same asymmetrical cross-rhythm noted in "Jolene."

Returning to the guitar riff in "Jolene," a secondary cross-rhythm involves the bass notes on beats 1 through 3 and the individual melody units in the first two motives (example 3.4). (Listen to examples 3.8 and 3.9 ▶.) This additional cross-rhythm is a four-against-three polyrhythm: the first four melodic units (each the duration of a dotted eighth note) move against the first three bass notes. As noted above, the melody and bass metrically realign on the fourth beat.

EXAMPLE 3.3 Banjo rolls: forward roll and backward roll in notation and tablature, open G tuning.

Top two lines, notated with symmetrical groupings; counting numbers above.

Middle line, the resultant asymmetrical cross-rhythm.

Bottom two lines, notated with asymmetrical groupings.

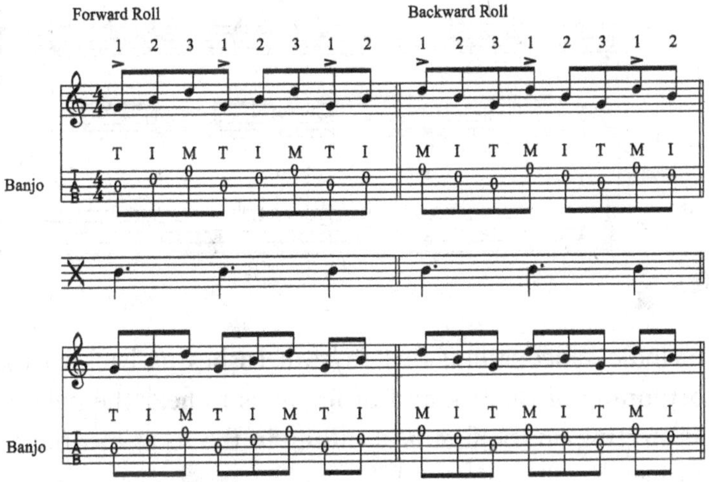

Of course, all this rhythmic complexity sails by at a quick 110 beats per minute. What registers, however, is the restless quality created by the tensions between the four even beats in the bass and the primary asymmetric cross-rhythm and the four-against-three polyrhythm of the melody. Kate Heidemann describes these rhythms as "anticipatory" and "hurried."[23] Within the polyrhythm, each of the melodic units (the four dotted eighth notes) do feel as though they each arrive a sixteenth note early. This rushing quality is intensified on beat 4 where the primary cross-rhythm note value is a quarter note, a shorter duration than the previous two dotted-quarter notes of the primary cross-rhythm. Second, this seemingly shortened fourth beat includes a

EXAMPLE 3.4 Dolly Parton, "Jolene" (1974), guitar lick, secondary cross-rhythm of four-against-three polyrhythm indicated.

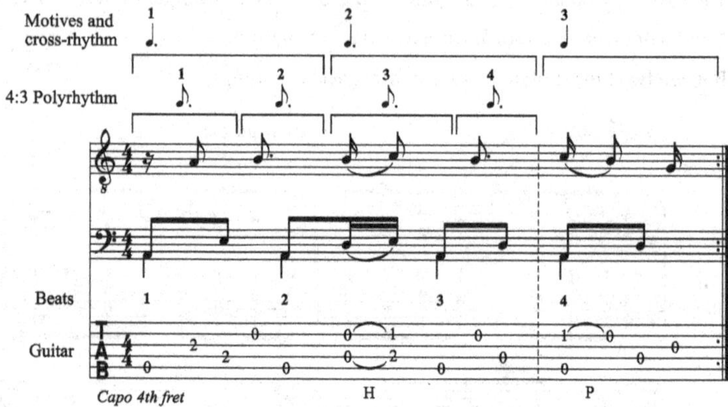

melodic syncopation; this rhythm rushes us back to the beginning of the lick and prompts us to hear the melody as starting on the first beat, filling in the A, as mentioned earlier.

It may be surprising that such a powerful and complicated riff does not appear in an instrumental solo after this intro. But it does not disappear. It is the undercurrent throughout "Jolene" that frequently links the end of one phrase with the beginning of another and gives Dolly a momentary breather throughout the song.

CHORUS

When asked why she thought "Jolene" was so beloved, Dolly said part of its appeal is "because it's just the same word over and over, even a first-grader or a baby can sing,

'Jolene, Jolene, Jolene, Jolene.' It's like, how hard can that be?"[24] Yes, who hasn't sung along to the chorus like two-year-old Sophia Kingsley, whose video went viral in 2017? (View example 3.10 ▶.)[25]

Pivoting from the guitar riff to the chorus and verses, remember that "Jolene" is in C♯ minor. The chorus is four lines long. Over the course of the first and third lines (on the name *Jolene*), the melody rises from the 1st scale degree ($\hat{1}$ tonic) to the upper tonic ($\hat{8}$) an octave higher and immediately falls back to the 5th scale degree (figure 3.2). From there, the second and fourth lines fall back to tonic. The effect is a question and answer, or, more precisely, a cry and a resigned plea: "an assertive rise and doomed, acquiescent fall."[26]

Calling out Jolene's name four times in this way creates a sense of urgency. Further, the chorus breaks away from

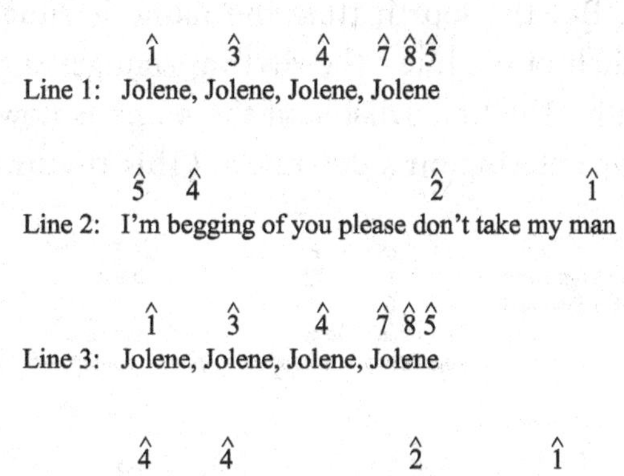

FIGURE 3.2 Dolly Parton, "Jolene," melodic outline of chorus, lines 1 and 2; structural notes only; the melody of lines 3 and 4 is identical to lines 1 and 2.

the hold that the tonic had during the guitar intro, and the harmonic rhythm accelerates. Each time Jolene's name is sung, the chord changes, which intensifies the singer's pleas (figure 3.3). Starting with the minor tonic (i), the next chord brightens the line with the relative major (III). Heading into the end of the line, Dolly sings the third *Jolene* on a ♭VII chord (Dolly's "sorrow chord"), which then resolves on the tonic (i) on the last *Jolene*. Lines two and four of the chorus prolong the ♭VII chord and only return to tonic at the end of the line. The singer's unrelenting pleas are repeated in lines 3 and 4 of the chorus with the same chord progression and melody.

The rhythm of the chorus further adds to the insistency of the singer's appeal to Jolene. The first three iterations of "Jolene" begin on an upbeat, which makes musical and poetic sense. After all, the name *Jolene* has the accent on the second syllable, so a short-LONG rhythm is suited to Jo-LENE. But the fourth time the name is sung—at the highest pitch of the line—the rhythm changes slightly but significantly. The first syllable of the name is now equally stressed by entering on a downbeat. (This rhythm—going

Chords:	c#	E	B	c#
Roman Numeral System, c#:	i	III	♭VII	i
Nashville Number System, E:	6-	1	5	6-
Chorus lyrics:	Jolene,	Jolene,	Jolene,	Jolene
Verse lyrics:	Your beauty is beyond compare with flaming locks of auburn hair			

Chords:	B	c#
Roman Numeral System:	♭VII	i
Nashville Number System:	5	6-
Chorus lyrics:	I'm begging of you please don't take my man	
Verse lyrics:	With ivory skin and eyes of emerald green	

FIGURE 3.3 Dolly Parton, "Jolene," identical chord progression in chorus and verse, first lines.

from three upbeat gestures to one downbeat gesture—also evokes the guitar lick, with its first three syncopated, off-beat motives and its final motive that realigns with beat 4.) In the chorus, the singer starts out trying hard to get Jolene's attention through repetition, speech-like rhythm, rising pitch levels, and new chords, and the final *Jolene* is the most emphatic, seeming to demand that she listen.

VERSES

The verses are linked to the chorus through the same "great chord progression,"[27] as Dolly calls it (figure 3.3). Each verse is six lines long and divides into two identical three-line segments each in the musical form a a′ b.[28]

Verse	**Chorus (for comparison of form)**
Segment 1:	
Line 1 a Your beauty is beyond compare	Jolene, Jolene
Line 2 a′ With flaming locks of auburn hair	Jolene, Jolene
Line 3 b With ivory skin and eyes of emerald green	I'm begging of you . . .
Segment 2:	
Line 4 a Your smile is like a breath of spring	Jolene, Jolene
Line 5 a′ Your voice is soft like summer rain	Jolene, Jolene
Line 6 b And I cannot compete with you Jolene	Please don't take him . . .

Further, the melodic contour of the verses is like that of the chorus. In each segment of the verses, the melody rises in the first two lines and returns to the tonic in the third line (figure 3.4). But the highest note reached is only the 5th scale degree (at the ends of lines 2 and 5), rather than the upper tonic as in the chorus. This more limited range is appropriate for the part of the song that is wordy and

$\hat{1}$ $\hat{3}$ $\hat{4}$ $\hat{5}$

Line 1: Your beauty is beyond compare with flaming locks of auburn hair

$\hat{5}$ $\hat{4}$ $\hat{2}$ $\hat{1}$

Line 2: With ivory skin and eyes of emerald green

FIGURE 3.4 Dolly Parton, "Jolene," melodic outline of verses, lines 1 and 2; structural notes only; the melody of lines 3 and 4 is identical to lines 1 and 2.

speech-like. The ascent to the upper tonic is better reserved for the pleading lines of the chorus when the singer can only repeat Jolene's name.

Finally, as in the chorus, the name *Jolene* is prominent in the verses. Dolly uses it as a refrain at the end of each phrase with one exception: the first phrase of the first verse ends with *green* instead of *Jolene*. Unlike the chorus, however, the verses are packed with words. In the same length of time it takes to sing one utterance of *Jolene* in the chorus, Dolly sings up to five words/syllables in the verses, as if the singer is breathlessly arguing her case.

Turning to the poetic structure of the verses, Dolly mirrors the musical form (a a′ b a a′ b) with the rhyme scheme aab ccb. In the second and third verses, the rhymes are perfect (or nearly so) and sometimes identical: *sleep/keep/Jolene*, *understand/man/Jolene*, *men/again/Jolene*, *you/you/Jolene*. Also noteworthy is her approach in verse 2. Dolly uses a well-placed enjambment (at "keep/from crying") as well as incremental repetition ("I can easily" and "you could easily") to strengthen the forward momentum.

This aab ccb rhyme scheme, however, is not followed precisely in the first verse. Some of the rhymes are imperfect, creating an ambiguous rhyme scheme: *compare/hair/*

green, spring/rain/Jolene. The rhymes could be stretched a bit to be heard as aab ccb like the other verses by linking *green/Jolene* as the two b rhymes and allowing the imperfect rhyme of *spring/rain* to form the two c lines. However, one could also hear it as aab bcc by linking the imperfect chain rhyme of *green/spring* and the imperfect rhyme *rain/ Jolene.* Another option is aab bcb, with *green/spring/Jolene* as the b rhyme. The stronger rhyme here is *green/Jolene,* with *green* in the refrain place of *Jolene* in line three of the first verse.

My aim is not to figure out which option is correct; instead, the ambiguity is the point. This first verse is the most notable one in the song for good reason. It is the most picturesque and vibrant. Here Dolly sacrifices poetic rigidity in the rhymes to more freely portray Jolene's beauty. And the flexibility of the rhymes, especially the *green/ spring* chain rhyme, bridges this verse's first and second halves and intensifies the rhapsodic onrush of words.

PHRASE AND FORMAL STRUCTURE

Dolly also captures a breathless, imploring atmosphere in "Jolene" by manipulating the pace of the song through phrase extensions and the meta-rhythm of chorus and verses. She varies the phrase lengths of the verses and chorus, often extending them beyond the expected length of four measures. In the chorus, Dolly adds an extra measure after singing Jolene's name in the first and third phrases. Below is a comparison of the phrase lengths; each number is a measure. In the top line, the count is given with a standard four-bar phrase (be careful not to pause or add a beat after 4). The lower line shows the measure count as Dolly composed it (do not rush through the 5; count that as evenly as the first four counts).

Jo-LENE	Jo-LENE	Jo-LENE	JO-LENE	I'm begging . . .	
1	2	3	4	1	
Jo-LENE	Jo-LENE	Jo-LENE	JO-LENE		I'm begging . . .
1	2	3	4	5	1

Does the singer need that extra time to collect herself after calling out to Jolene? Or perhaps the final, emphatic cry at the line's end needs a bit more time to resonate. Dolly also extends the second and fourth phrases of the chorus two extra measures, following the plea for Jolene not to take her man. This gives the singer even more breathing room, which the guitar often fills in with its signature lick, as noted above.

For the verses, Dolly further exploits the different phrase lengths (figure 3.5). Here she takes no extra time between

Intro							
	6-	6-	6-	6-			One time through the lick spans two counts of 6-;
	6-	6-	6-	6-			thus, the lick is played four times
Chorus							
	6-	1	5	6-	**6-**		Jolene, Jolene, Jolene, Jolene
	5	5	6-	6-	**6-**	**6-**	I'm begging of you please …
	6-	1	5	6-	**6-**		Jolene, Jolene, Jolene, Jolene
	5	5	6-	6-	**6-**	**6-**	Please don't take him…
Verse							
	6-	1	5	6-			Your beauty is beyond compare…
	5	5	6-	6-	**6-**	**6-**	With ivory skin and eyes of…
	6-	1	5	6-			Your voice is like a breath…
	5	5	6-	6-	**6-**	**6-**	And I cannot compete with you…

FIGURE 3.5 Sample studio chart of "Jolene," intro, verse, and chorus; Nashville system chords and phrase structure. The bold chords indicate the phrase extensions. This is not a full working chart, but an outline of the structure of each section of the song showing the phrase extensions.

the a and a′ lines of each segment. The words rush through these two lines with no room to breathe until she reaches the name *Jolene* (or, in the case of the first verse, the word *green*). At this point, Dolly adds the same two-measure extension as in lines 2 and 4 of the chorus, and the guitar again often comes forward to fill in the space between the first and second halves of the verses. The guitar returns for another two-measure extension at the end of each verse, propelling us to the next section. These added spaces give the listener time to contemplate the singer's plea and the reasons for it, which deepen our understanding of her feelings.

In addition to varying the phrase lengths, which engenders interest at the local level, Dolly also shapes the overall form of the song so that it is not predictable. She starts with the hook of the guitar intro that moves seamlessly into the chorus. She then front-loads the first two verses in the song, and the words pour from her. She describes her rival in detail in the first verse. Then, in a run-on maneuver, she continues to the second verse, with no chorus for a breather, where she explains the effect Jolene has on her man and the seeming inevitability of Jolene's victory.[29] Only now does the chorus return, once more imploring Jolene not to take her man. The third verse seems short in comparison to what has come before. In its six lines Dolly concludes by stating that Jolene will be the one who determines the outcome. The final chorus seems to appear ahead of schedule, as though the singer has no more arguments to make—there is nothing left to do but continue to plead with Jolene. The song ends almost abruptly with a brief coda as Dolly sings Jolene's name twice more: once on a single low tonic note, and then up an octave and decorated with the kind of turning ornament that is part of her signature vocal style. At that, the song quickly fades out.

Heidemann observes that the song's asymmetric phrase and formal structure outlined here is also "a modern take on the asymmetrical, improvisatory, and text-dependent phrasing practices present in much traditional, old-time music of the 1930s, such as the ballads and hymns recorded by the Carter Family."[30] Heard in this context, Dolly's musical choices about form not only reflect the pleading in the lyrics, but also reveal her reliance on old-world sounds that our musical analysis began with.

SOMETHING OLD AND SOMETHING NEW

Even as Dolly saturated "Jolene" with old-world resonances, she created an innovative sound that she had wanted to explore for a long time: "That was the first time I noticed people sayin', 'That's different than what you been doin'.' But I had been fightin' for that sort of thing for years. I had all these songs I was writin', and I was developin' musically, as far as a different style of pickin' and hearin' different sounds in my mind was concerned. 'Jolene' was the first good example of the fact that you can be yourself and still improve on whatever you do."[31] It is unclear what Dolly thought was different about "Jolene." Perhaps it was the minor, old-world sound. But it may have been something more practical: its crossover potential.

Dolly started moving into the pop world in the mid-1970s, and the inclusion of the bongo in the instrumental mix of "Jolene" added "a modern, cosmopolitan element to the . . . rustic imagery."[32] Nine months after Dolly's recording of "Jolene" topped the *Billboard* Country Chart, her light, pop song "Love Is Like a Butterfly" did the same. Five years after "Jolene," when Dolly had unequivocally become a pop star, critic Noel Coppage wrote that Dolly could no longer compose songs like the early folk-inspired "Coat of Many Colors" or "her middle-period, still modal influenced ones like 'Jolene' . . . and expect to do what she wants to do."[33] By the time of Coppage's lament in 1979, Dolly had been on the pop chart with several more songs, including her "hot as a pistol" hit "Baby I'm Burnin'" (1978) with its disco vibe. And by then, she was a long way from "Jolene."

PART II

COVERS OF "JOLENE"

CHAPTER 4

OLIVIA NEWTON-JOHN'S "JOLENE"

THE FIRST PROMINENT COVER of "Jolene" came from an unlikely performer in 1976. (Listen to example 4.1 ▶.) British-Australian pop singer Olivia Newton-John had a complicated, uneasy relationship with the country music world in the mid-1970s. At that time, Nashville was worried that pop music and musicians were infiltrating country music. Newton-John was a catalyst for action in this battle about the identity of country music entertainers. Her version of "Jolene" was released in the midst of this divisive reckoning, and it appeared the year Dolly signed with new management and began her own move into pop music in earnest. Dolly had a front-row seat during the brouhaha in Nashville where she witnessed Newton-John's growing presence in country music and her success with a pop-style

Dolly Parton's Jolene. Lydia R. Hamessley, Oxford University Press.
DOI: 10.1093/9780197760345.003.0005

"Jolene," which figured in Dolly's thinking about her own potential as a pop star. The song eventually became a vehicle for their touching collaboration just before Newton-John's death.

NEWTON-JOHN GOES COUNTRY AND THE ASSOCIATION OF COUNTRY ENTERTAINERS

Newton-John's cover of "Jolene" was not her first foray into country music. Two of her hit singles oozed pop country with prominent steel guitar, lively two-stepping tempos and rhythms, and gospel-inspired vocals. In the fall of 1973, she won a Grammy for Best Country Vocal Performance, Female for "Let Me Be There." In 1974, "If You Love Me Let Me Know" went to #5 on the *Billboard* Hot 100 Chart and #2 on the Country Chart. (Listen to examples 4.2 and 4.3 ▶.) Her record label took out full-page ads in country music magazines, portraying her as a rising country music star (figure 4.1). But what shocked many in Nashville was that Newton-John was named the Country Music Association Female Vocalist of the Year for 1974, winning the award over Dolly Parton, Loretta Lynn, Anne Murray, and Tanya Tucker.

Incensed at Newton-John's win, several prominent country stars met at the estate of Tammy Wynette and George Jones and formed the Association of Country Entertainers (ACE). Bill Anderson, the first chair of ACE, explained that the issues about country music losing its identity had been roiling for some time but that Newton-John was "the straw that broke the camel's back."[1] Johnny Paycheck said, "We're not against pop records. We're not

FIGURE 4.1 Olivia Newton-John ad from *Country Music* magazine (July 1974), 31, three months before her CMA award for Female Vocalist of the Year. "The girl who won this year's Grammy for Best Female Country Artist, as well as the Academy of Country Music's Most Promising Female Vocalist award [in 1973]. . . . 'Let Me Be There' is the song that won her the country music accolades earlier this year."

against the Olivia Newton-Johns. But we are for country entertainment."[2] Other members were not so circumspect. Billy Walker complained of big money "outside influences" from the East and West coasts: "We are mainly people who made country music what it is today, trying to protect our business because we see it flaking off in thousands of directions. We're trying to keep it at home."[3] "These people came in and prostituted our business and watered down our music."[4] Barbara Mandrell, also an ACE board member, tempered these types of comments, saying: "This group was not started out of jealousy. I'm a big fan of Olivia Newton-John, but she isn't country."[5]

ACE limited its membership "strictly to those who make their living as country music entertainers." Anderson said ACE "is making no effort to precisely define country music, but rather will screen its membership by asking where an artist places his allegiance."[6] This screening committee originally included Dolly, but she was not deeply involved in the group.

For her part, Newton-John stayed out of the fray. Earlier in 1974, prior to the CMA Awards, she said that she had been lucky to get the country audience with her "easygoing, country-tilted style thing. . . . I think I'm accepted by country people, but I don't think people think of me as strictly country."[7] After her CMA win, she offered a gracious response in a pre-taped acceptance speech: "It's a long way from London to Nashville, but I'd like to take this opportunity to say a big hello to all the friends I made on my last visit there. And I hope to see you all soon when I fulfill an ambition of mine to record an album in your hometown."[8] A few months after the dust-up in Nashville, she said, "It has nothing to do with me. I've never claimed to be a country singer; to call yourself that, you'd have to be born in that background. I simply love country music and its straightforwardness. And since the records have also sold well outside of the country audience, it seems to me that we're broadening the acceptance for country music. I wasn't out to do anybody out of an award."[9] She later said she had been a "scapegoat. . . . A lot of people are listening to country music because of me. You don't have to live in Nashville to sing or like country music."[10]

NEWTON-JOHN'S "JOLENE"

It was in this climate that Newton-John recorded her version of "Jolene" for her album *Come On Over*, released in 1976 and recorded in late 1975, just a year after the CMA controversy. The album went to #2 on *Billboard*'s Top Country Albums Chart. It also included "Blue Eyes Crying in the Rain" and the traditional song "Greensleeves." (Listen to examples 4.4 and 4.5 ▶.) The title song "Come On Over" performed better on *Billboard*'s Country Chart (at #5) than it did on the Hot 100 Chart (at #23). (Listen to example 4.6 ▶.)

Newton-John's "Jolene" begins with a syncopated acoustic guitar riff as in Dolly's recording. The familiar agitated energy and polyrhythmic intensity of the original is there. Yet something is different. The riff in Dolly's version oscillates between the 2nd and 3rd scale degrees. Newton-John's ratchets up the urgency by transferring the rocking melody up to the 4th and 5th scale degrees. Just when your ear recognizes the iconic riff and your eyebrows raise at the unexpected higher melody—as you lean in to figure out what is different, expecting to hear the pattern four times—an electric guitar takes over after two patterns to finish the intro. Here is a more urgent driving rhythm, edgy and shifting the frame of reference with an accompanying whooshing sound effect of disco. The acoustic guitar riff is still present but subsumed under this new electric guitar line that is now melodically dominant. This new riff will appear throughout the song, marking the ends of phrases as in Dolly's original. Even before Newton-John sings, the instrumentals take this "Jolene" into the realm of pop and disco.

The recording showcases Newton-John's vocal agility, particularly in the song's extended coda, which parts with the original structure. Dolly's coda is short; she ends by singing *Jolene* two times after the final chorus. But instead of ending this way, Newton-John sings *Jolene* eight times with rhapsodic vocals that place melismas (strings of notes) on the final syllable: *Jo-**lene*** (2:25) (example 4.1). Most of the melismas are four notes (those marked, 1, 2, 4, and 6), but the third melisma is ten notes long (the tempo increases slightly at that point), and the fifth melisma is six notes long (and goes to the highest note of the song). Her vocal prowess is on full display as she soars higher and higher, blissfully extending the lines.

Newton-John begins the coda on the upper tonic and sings "Jolene" three times (melismas 1, 2, and 3) as she works her way down through the lower octave. Along the way she introduces the raised 6th scale degree in the second melisma (C♮, which, in e♭ minor, suggests the Dorian mode). This first half of the coda ends with her longest

EXAMPLE 4.1 Olivia Newton-John, "Jolene" coda (1976), eight melismas indicated.

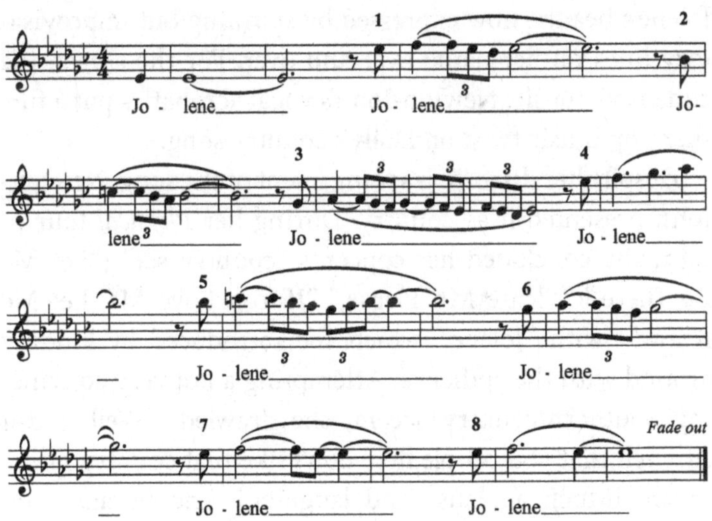

melisma and could have signaled the end of the song. But she goes back for more by moving immediately back to the upper tonic. From there she soars up to her highest note, C♮, the raised 6th scale degree (melisma 5). After that, she echoes her previous descent through thc octave (melisma 6), though now in the upper range. She then signals the song's conclusion and waning energy by twice shortening the melismas to just two notes (melismas 7 and 8).

At this point, the song quickly begins to fade out. But if you listen closely, you can hear Newton-John again return to the top of her range, and her last audible notes are in the upper octave with the high C♮. It is easy to imagine that Newton-John continues to sing higher and higher, just out of range of our hearing. This extended coda on Jolene's name places the performer in two positions. For the song's narrator, the melismas enhance the song's pleading quality while also musically embodying the rhapsodic lyrics to Jolene's beauty, now expressed by spinning out improvisatory lines on her name over and over. For the singer, the coda is virtuosic. Newton-John's vocal acrobatics put a further pop music twist on Dolly's country song.

Despite her disco/pop arrangement of the song, Newton-John presented it as country. During her *Physical* tour in 1982, she concluded her concert's "country set" ("Let Me Be There," "Please Mr. Please," "If You Love Me, Let Me Know") with "Jolene," which she introduced by kidding around with the audience. Attempting a not very convincing Southern/country accent, she drawled, "Well, I can sure tell that you people here don't like that country music much. [Much applause and laughter.] And because you don't like it so much, I'm gonna sing another one for you right now."[11] (View example 4.7 ▶.)

DOLLY'S RESPONSE

Newton-John's biographer Tim Ewbank reports that she recorded "Jolene" to thank Dolly for supporting her after the ACE controversy,[12] and Newton-John acknowledged Dolly's kindness in her autobiography.[13] Although Dolly had been involved in ACE, she was not pulled into the controversy, saying: "It doesn't make any difference to me because all the country people are trying to go pop and all the pop people are trying to go country. So whoever wins, I figure it's equal."[14]

In 1977, Newton-John won the Favorite Female Artist-Pop/Rock at the American Music Awards (her third win in a row). Since she could not attend the ceremony, she asked Dolly to accept the award for her. At the podium that night, Dolly affirmed that there was no rift between the two singers: "I'm real real proud of this. I'm happy to say that Olivia and I are friends, and she asked me if I would do this. Maybe one of these days she can come and accept one for me if I ever get that hot. But thanks for Olivia. She'd love you all for this. I know she would."[15]

Newton-John's award recognized her two albums from 1976, *Come On Over* and *Don't Stop Believin'*. Dolly was certainly aware that part of Newton-John's success—she was "hot" and Dolly was not—was Newton-John's disco/pop cover of "Jolene" on *Come On Over*. That album went to #2 on the Country Chart and #13 on the *Billboard* Hot 200 Chart. Its release in March 1976 was followed in June by a strong appearance on the UK and Irish charts of Dolly's original recording of "Jolene" that had recently been released as a single in the UK. It was Dolly's first top ten song in the UK. In June, Dolly's "Jolene" peaked at #7 on the Official UK Top 40 chart and #8 on the Irish chart, spending six weeks on each.

Always mindful she was in the music *business*, Dolly took note of Newton-John's success with "Jolene" and the boost it gave her own recording. The song was more than a renewed moneymaker. Its revived popularity was another indication for Dolly that she should follow her instincts and embrace a pop style to achieve her goal of being a superstar. To do this, in 1976 Dolly signed with Sandy Gallin of the LA-based management firm Katz, Gallin & Cleary, which also managed Olivia Newton-John. That year Dolly hosted a thirty-minute television variety show, *Dolly!* Of course, she performed "Jolene" on one of the episodes, but on another she opened the show singing Newton-John's hit, "Let Me Be There."

In 1977, Dolly recorded her first self-produced album, *New Harvest . . . First Gathering*, which included the song "You Are." (Listen to example 4.9 ▶.) Music critic John Rockwell of *The New York Times* called the song "a breathy, talking love ballad that builds to a rhetorical, sentimental climax and should effortlessly win for Miss Parton, Miss Newton-John's pop audience."[16]

Dolly's next album *Here You Come Again*, also from 1977, went even further into pop. Her new manager wanted to open the album with the pop crossover/countrypolitan title song. Dolly initially resisted—"I don't want to scare my audience to death"—but trusted Gallin's star-making skills. Besides, she was tired of not cashing in on her own talent and songs, and "Jolene" was a prime example: "I had a lot of trouble dealing with the resistance to my crossover from the old-timers in Nashville. To me it was simple arithmetic. 'Jolene' had been a number-one song in the country market and had only sold sixty thousand records. A hit on the pop charts could sell millions."[17] She and Gallin were right: "Here You Come Again" went to #1 on the Country Chart and #3 on the Hot 100 Chart. (Listen to example 4.10 ▶.) Both the song and the album were certified Platinum.

The ACE controversy had arisen because Newton-John was named CMA Entertainer of the Year in 1974. Four years later, Dolly won the same accolade following her chart-topping hit "Here You Come Again," a song written not by herself, but by Barry Mann and Cynthia Weil, the

Brill Building songwriting team who also co-wrote songs like "You've Lost That Lovin' Feeling" and "Somewhere Out There." By 1978, Nashville had embraced a pop crossover sound, and Dolly's countrypolitan song was country enough. Dolly noted the irony: "When 'Here You Come Again' was a big hit with country audiences too, I felt completely vindicated. . . . I helped to make a whole segment of society change the way they thought about country music and country singers. Now Nashville began to respond a little differently to me. When I was nominated by the CMA as Entertainer of the Year, it was a sure sign that Nashville had finally gotten over my crossover."[18]

In 1978, Dolly spoke with Lawrence Grobel of *Playboy* about her move into pop music in the context of covers by other artists. She said, "I've had tons of songs and albums recorded by other people. But I've yet to have that big, smash, 1,000,000-selling song of my own. I've had lots of number-one songs, but when you get involved in how much they sell, it's rare to get a 1,000,000 seller."[19] Dolly was comparing her relative lack of success with her songs to the successes of pop singers, some of whom were covering her songs. She mentioned that "Jolene," her biggest hit, gained even more popularity when Newton-John covered it. She also pointed to Linda Ronstadt's cover of "I Will Always Love You." Of course, this was fourteen years before Whitney Houston's recording of "I Will Always Love You" garnered Dolly $10 million in royalties in the 1990s.[20]

Dolly once said about Newton-John's cover of "Jolene": "It's one of the better things that's been done with my songs."[21] She meant, of course, that she liked its arrangement and Newton-John's performance. But Newton-John's "Jolene" was also important for Dolly as she did the calculations about her own crossover into pop.

OLIVIA AND DOLLY'S DUET

Dolly always had kind words for Newton-John, and in 2022 they finally had the opportunity to record together. The last project that Newton-John did was an album of duets, which included "Jolene." She and Dolly recorded the song a few months before Newton-John died on August 8, 2022, when Dolly recalled, "my first memory of Olivia was when her song 'Let Me Be There' was a hit. I have loved her ever since."[22]

Their duet blends the two women's approach to the song, with the instrumental intro introducing each singer's version in turn. (View and listen to examples 4.11a and 4.11b ▶.) First up is Dolly's acoustic guitar riff. In Newton-John's 1976 cover, the riff was shifted up in pitch (from the 2nd and 3rd scale degrees to the 4th and 5th). But here, the guitar remains at the original pitch level of Dolly's lick, which plays for the first half of the intro. Then, the electric guitar takes over and plays the same aggressive, driving rhythm and melody for the second half, as in Newton-John's cover. In this duet, the more folk-like version of Dolly's original joins the pop/disco version of Newton-John's cover, and the singers meet in the middle. Gone are the bongos of Dolly's recording, now replaced by the insistent backbeat of the drums. There is no sign of the disco whooshing that accompanied Newton-John. Their styles meld.

Both singers are in excellent form on the recording. Newton-John's high range is strong and clear, with the same vocal flip and high melodic embellishments that she used in her cover. Dolly's gift for melodic variation is on full display. Their voices complement each other, always individually distinctive, yet blending nicely, and they trade off singing the lead throughout. The song is Dolly's, much of the arrangement is Newton-John's, but the result is theirs equally.

The significant innovation in this duet is in the coda (example 4.2), which is based on the one in Newton-John's 1976 cover (example 4.1). Dolly and Newton-John begin by singing *Jolene* twice on the lower tonic, once in harmony and then once echoed by Dolly (2:23). What comes next is remarkable. Newton-John sings the same melismatic lines from her cover's coda. But now, the first three melismas are harmonized in three parts and in parallel motion, which imparts an archaic vibe. Newton-John's lines from her cover are the inner voice; she overdubs the lower and higher harmony lines. For her part, Dolly punctuates these lines with interjections on "Jolene." After these three melismas return to the lower tonic, the real fun begins. Newton-John sings her lines in the stratosphere—melismas 4, 5, and 6 from her cover version and an added seventh melisma—while Dolly stitches lines together from different verses.

Dolly's melodies for these lyrics are not from the song. She swings up and down the octave, singing new melodies in a speech-like, patter rhythm based on, but not identical to, the rhythms of the original lines. Her phrases feel improvised underneath Newton-John's soaring lines: Dolly recaps the story as Newton-John floats above it all, singing

EXAMPLE 4.2 Olivia Newton-John and Dolly Parton duet, "Jolene" coda (2023), seven melismas indicated.

Jolene's name over and over. As they bring the coda to a close, they do not fade out. Instead, there is a drive to the final cadence as Newton-John sings a new, seventh melisma to accommodate Dolly's last improvised line before they merge (after some delicious dissonance) an octave apart on

Jolene's name. Dolly then allows her voice to drop down to the lower 5th scale degree, which creates a hollow emotional effect. Each singer showcases her style in this complex counterpoint, and the polyphonic melding of the two singer's lines is breathtaking.

When they recorded the duet, Newton-John said she had always wanted to sing with Dolly. Blending their two approaches to "Jolene" was an inspired way for them to finally sing together. After Newton-John's death, Dolly said, "My last memory of Olivia was when I sang with her on my song 'Jolene' which she recorded for an album not so very long ago. I cannot wait to hear that album and Olivia may you rest in peace. You left a spot that one else will ever fill."

Dolly and Newton-John came from different musical worlds, but their paths crossed in significant ways for each of them. As Newton-John's publicist observed about their duet on "Jolene," it "seems like the perfect bookend to their decades-long friendship. Knowing that Dolly was there at the start of Olivia's US Country music career and here she is, one half of a duet of Olivia's final recording, is pretty special."[23]

CHAPTER 5

NEW PERSPECTIVES ON "JOLENE"

THERE ARE NOT MANY people who talk about Dolly's weakness as a songwriter. But Clarence Selman did in 1973:

> Her major weakness as a writer is that she has so stylized her songs by the time she's written them, that it would lead another artist to believe that they're only for Dolly Parton. The only genuine way for her to get around that is to deliberately write a song for another artist. . . . She has an automatic record for anything she writes, because she's her own vehicle. But as a writer, I think she should hope her songs are for everybody.[1]

Selman wrote this before "I Will Always Love You" and "Jolene" were released, so perhaps we can forgive his misstep. These two songs are "for everybody," so much so that

Dolly Parton's Jolene. Lydia R. Hamessley, Oxford University Press. © Oxford University Press 2025.
DOI: 10.1093/9780197760345.003.0006

until the most recent "Dolly moment," most people likely did not know she wrote and recorded "I Will Always Love You" and only knew the song through Whitney Houston's legendary cover. And "Jolene" is one of Dolly's most covered songs. Jim Beviglia has a point that, despite all the "Jolene" covers out there, "no one has brought her to life quite like Dolly Parton, the songwriter who created her."[2] However, there are numerous versions of "Jolene" by artists who make the song their own.[3] Examples range from the Scottish duo Strawberry Switchblade's new wave/pop version (1985) to Rhonda Vincent's bluegrass version (2000), and from the Wellington International Ukulele Orchestra, New Zealand (2009), to Destructo's EDM remix (2021).

One website lists over 240 versions and adaptations, with the majority dating from 2000 to 2024 (figure 5.1).[4] I limit my discussion to six examples, some familiar and some lesser known. I first examine a recording by Mindy

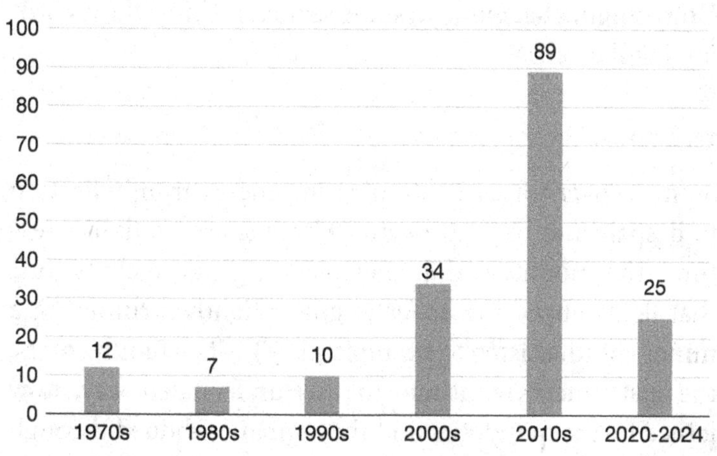

FIGURE 5.1 Number of "Jolene" covers, 1973–2024.

Smith that was purported to be Dolly's favorite.[5] I then consider examples in which artists reimagine the world of the song through new lenses that help them identify with the song's assumed white, female narrator: covers by The White Stripes, Lil Nas X, The Congo Cowboys, Gloria Ann Taylor, and Chiquis Rivera and Becky G.

MINDY SMITH

From 1999 to 2002, Dolly recorded three bluegrass albums.[6] The first two were produced by Steve Buckingham, who soon after produced a tribute album in Dolly's honor, *Just Because I'm a Woman: Songs of Dolly Parton* (2003). It included Mindy Smith's version of "Jolene," which seemed to draw on the mountain music atmosphere that Dolly and Buckingham had recently explored. Shortly after this tribute album, Smith released the song on her album *One Moment More* (2004). For that recording, Buckingham took Smith's tribute album version and mixed in new tracks of Dolly singing harmony in some sections. This is the recording I will discuss.

THE SONG

Smith's cover traces a path of rising energy from reflection to despair and back. It begins with a sparse, folk-like texture. The mountain dulcimer plays a gentle melodic line that floats above the acoustic guitar lightly strumming a minor chord. (Listen to example 5.1 ▶.) When Smith enters, the instruments continue in this understated way, now joined by the mandolin, and they remain subdued through the first chorus and first verse. As the second verse begins, the instruments come slightly forward in the texture, and the percussion is more audible. With the next chorus, the vibe gets edgier (1:20). It retains an "old-world" flavor but now is draped in a contemporary setting with the addition of distorted electric guitar and percussion. At the chorus's last line, Dolly herself enters the song, singing harmony, including an open fifth at the cadence that contributes to the archaic feel.

After this second chorus, there is a more energetic, improvisational instrumental section, dominated by the rock-inflected electric guitar that does not reprise the melody of either the verse or the chorus (1:43). At the end of this section, which is the length of a chorus, the energy of the instrumentation suddenly dissipates as Smith sings verse 3 (2:04). The lyric "you could have your choice of men, but I could never love again" sounds defeated when sung to the same sparse accompaniment heard earlier. Dolly reappears in the middle of the verse as Smith finds her voice again at the line "I had to have this talk with you, whatever you decide to do, Jolene." Her plea to Jolene now sounds assertive, supported by the electric guitar.

This renewed energy continues through the next chorus. Dolly echoes each "Jolene" of lines 1 and 3 and joins Smith in harmony of lines 2 and 4. Line 2 also features a slight, but effective change in the melody. At the end of the lyric "please don't take my man," Smith does not let her voice drop back down to the tonic as she did in earlier choruses (and as Dolly does in the original). Instead, she stays on the 5th scale degree, singing with a strong, straight tone (2:38). Dolly matches Smith's raw sound as she sings her harmony lines with a similar straight tone. The effect is not that of a weak plea, but an insistent admonition, bolstered by Dolly's harmonies and intentionally forced vocal quality. At this point in the original, Dolly moved right to the coda. But Smith takes another pass through the chorus, repeating her strong cadence on the open-ended 5th scale degree (3:02). Dolly again echoes the name "Jolene," and, rather than singing line 2 in harmony, she sings an improvisatory response at the end of the line.

When Smith sings "Jolene, Jolene, Jolene, Jolene" for the final time, Dolly joins her on the last *Jolene*, which they hold for six extra beats (3:08). The rock inflection in the song fades as the instruments all but drop out at this point, only vamping lightly to mark time. Is this a final cry for mercy? Or a final warning? Like the original, the answer is ambiguous. Smith then sings the last line alone to minimal accompaniment. The instruments return for the coda (3:18), which reprises their haunting improvisations from the intro. Smith lightly sings "Jolene" only once before she hums along with the band, and they all continue to explore, in an almost trance-like state, the musical space of the song as if meditating on the situation. Dolly adds to this effect by making a final ghostly appearance as well. The song's long trajectory from introspection to desperation and back is enhanced by Dolly's presence. She enters the song subtly, sneaking in at the end of the second chorus. Her voice adds gravitas to the third chorus, her presence fades a bit in the fourth chorus, and her voice barely registers in the coda as the energy of the song dissipates.

In Smith's version, there is no sign of Dolly's signature guitar lick to kick off the song. Often in covers of "Jolene," artists do not replicate the lick exactly. But they still usually come up with something similar in its place, something that has the same driving rhythm as Dolly's riff. To my ear, those attempts are often a disappointment. But Smith avoids this quandary by not offering an alternate riff. To be sure, her version has an instrumental intro, but with a very different vibe from Dolly's. Here, the instruments freely improvise, and the atmosphere feels less frantic, though no less anguished. This feeling is supported by Smith's melodic variants of Dolly's original vocal line. Small shifts of melody and rhythm stake out Smith's claim on Dolly's song as her own. Indeed, when Smith and Dolly sang the song on *The Tonight Show with Jay Leno* (2003),[7] Dolly was generous, completely giving herself over to the younger woman's vision for the song. (View example 5.2 ▶.)

THE MUSIC VIDEO

Dolly also participated in the music video for Smith's "Jolene," which is framed by her presence as the song's writer. The video is set to the recording on the tribute album *Just Because I'm a Woman: Songs of Dolly Parton* that does not include Dolly's voice. (View example 5.3 ▶.) As the scene opens, Dolly is seated outside a mountain cabin. With her guitar nearby, she opens a book and begins to write the lyrics of "Jolene." Intercut with these images are scenes of the Jolene story: a guy drives off in his car to meet another woman, leaving his partner (Smith) alone in a cabin. Dolly continues to write the story, but the video soon focuses on the cheating lover. He picks up Jolene, who appears as the second chorus begins, and they kiss passionately in his car. Eventually, Smith leaves the cabin and walks through the woods, carrying a lantern, searching for her partner.

The scene where she finds them in the car is powerful. During the six-beat extension of *Jolene* in the final chorus (3:08), Smith stands directly in front of the car, awash in the headlights. She and Jolene lock eyes, and Jolene seems ashamed and tries to look away. But Smith holds her with an impassive gaze that seems in equal parts accusatory, pleading, and defiant (especially at 3:25). The video then returns to Dolly, the songwriter. She closes the book that contains her lyrics and looks pensively skyward. Dolly often says when she writes songs, she sees them in her mind like she is watching a movie. This last shot of the video reminds us of that remark. The "Jolene" story, though covered by Smith, is Dolly's creation.

THE WHITE STRIPES, LIL NAS X, THE CONGO COWBOYS, AND GLORIA TAYLOR

THE WHITE STRIPES

The rock performance of "Jolene" by The White Stripes raises the question: what happens when a male singer covers the song? Of course, he can perform the song without identifying as the first-person narrator. Since "Jolene" is so firmly linked with Dolly, the song can stand on its own without the veneer of having to express the singer's authentic utterance. Or, as Jack White did in the cover by The White Stripes, the performer can reimagine the characters in the scenario.

White explained his approach: "I thought to take the character and change the context and make this red-headed woman my girlfriend, and that she's cheating on me with one of my friends. Then, that would be what I could really get emotionally attached to."[8] Thus, there is no need to make any changes in the lyrics in his garage-rock version (Listen to example 5.4 ▶.) After his opening guitar riff, he enters an octave higher than expected, and he seems desperate. He has abandoned all reason from the outset and is off kilter, undone by betrayal. In the first chorus and all the verses, he sounds broken, his voice raspy and torn. But in the following choruses, emotional and physical exhaustion is overcome by rage (or is it panic?) as he screams Jolene's name to the distorted fuzz of his guitar and amped up drums. This effect is stronger in the live recording than in the studio version. As Marissa Moss writes, "When he sings, 'please don't take him/even though you can,' not resorting to a gender swap, it doesn't matter if it's a male or a female howling—he tells the story loud and clear, and that's all that matters."[9]

LIL NAS X

If White's cover is overwrought, manic, and even deranged as he shrieks his heartbreak, Lil Nas X's performance of "Jolene" on the BBC Radio 1 Live Lounge (2021) is understated (View example 5.5 ▶.) Lil Nas described the song as "beautifully sad" and said that he likes the song's "little twang."[10] His honey-rich baritone voice dominates, sounding velvety and resigned—beautifully sad. He retains the gendered lyrics as White did, but now with a different implication: he sings "please don't take my man" as a Black gay man (figure 5.2).

FIGURE 5.2 Lil Nas X at BBC Radio 1 Live Lounge performance (2021).

The song begins with a single chord on the guitar, with no rhythmic riff here or anywhere in the song. The guitar plays only at the chord changes as Lil Nas sings the first chorus, which feels like an intro since it is sung in a slow, almost meterless, tempo. At the first verse, Lil Nas kicks up the tempo slightly, but the band does not yet fully join in as we might expect. Instead, the accompaniment remains minimal, with the guitar subtly supported by bass and very light percussion. At the second chorus, the band provides a bit more rhythmic activity, and the backup vocalists almost inaudibly sing with Lil Nas, but their parts are more for color than harmony. The drums finally make themselves known in the final verse and chorus. He ends by singing the line "please don't take him even though you can" three times, slowing down to the finish.

Cradling a rhinestone-covered mic attached to a stand decorated in flowers and with a butterfly (hello Dolly), Lil Nas sings "Jolene" as a queer song of heartbreak and abandonment. One commentator at the time pointed out that his performance occurred during Bisexual Awareness Week.[11] Another wrote, he "infuses the song with the struggles inherent to his identity as a gay Black man. The lyric 'I'm begging of you please don't take my man' is given powerful new meaning in the context of Lil Nas's own experiences with homophobia and marginalization."[12]

THE CONGO COWBOYS

The mountain music vibe that Mindy Smith's cover draws on is audible in the version by The Congo Cowboys, a South African–based band (figure 5.3). They reimagine American roots music "through Kwassa Kwassa African rhythms and Soukous guitar. The result is a gritty exploration of Americana and old-timey ditties, with a distinctly African twist."[13] The group features the banjo in their version of "Jolene," and their other recordings include old-time classics like "Pretty Polly," "Cluck Old Hen," and "Cuckoo" as well as new compositions sung in English and Lingala, one of the four national languages of the Democratic Republic of Congo.

FIGURE 5.3 The Congo Cowboys, l. to r., Simon Attwell (banjo), Chris Bakalanga (vocals and guitar), Julio Sigauque (bass). Courtesy of The Congo Cowboys.

There have been several US and European performers in the past decade or so who have made connections between the music of Appalachia and Africa and between the banjo and African instruments like the akonting, ngoni, and xalam. But, with their music, The Congo Cowboys trace the lineage of African music to Appalachia and back from a different perspective. They make the song their own by singing it, in their words, with an "African twist." Moreover, in their cover of "Jolene," The Congo Cowboys extend the Jolene story with added lyrics that create an unambiguous, unhappy outcome to the song's scenario. (Listen to example 5.6 ▶.)

Congolese singer Chris Bakalanga opens the song with the first line of the chorus sung in a slow, speech-like rhythm accompanied by guitar. Then the instrumental opening of the song begins on banjo, played in a clawhammer style. We are in Dolly's world, at least momentarily. But once the chorus proper begins, followed by verse 1, the full band plays, mixing in the African rhythms and timbres of the guitar and percussion. Also veering from Dolly's original, they alter some of the lyrics in verse 1 by omitting its racialized description of Jolene: red hair, green eyes, and ivory skin. Her charming smile and voice remain. Her beauty is celestial, and she is radiant.[14]

Kitoko nayo,	Your beauty,
Nako kokanisa yango na nini	There's nothing I can compare with
Okongenga lokola monzoto	You are shining like a star
Esekeli nayo bonzenga,	Your smile is gorgeous,
Mongongo nayo lokola	Your voice is like
Matanga ya nvula . . . Jolene	Soft rain . . . Jolene

After the chorus and verse 1, the band alters the form of the song. Rather than going directly into verse 2, the band sings another chorus (1:12) followed by an instrumental verse led by guitar (1:36). The band then sings verse 2 (1:57) and goes into another chorus (2:19). At this point, halfway through their performance, the band has already sung as many choruses as Dolly did in her original. And there are more changes to come.

Next, they add a fifty-second section that feels improvisatory. First, Bakalanga speaks lyrics in a free rhythm over a loose outline of the verse's/chorus's chord changes played by bass and guitar (2:42). Suddenly the driving rhythm of the banjo returns, joined by percussion and guitar

(3:16). The instruments lay down an ostinato over which Bakalanga speaks rhythmic lines of text.

Spoken section in free rhythm:

Kozanga pasi	To lose what your heart loves the most
Mingi mingi eloko oyo motema eluli	It's so painful
Nasala ko nini	What should I do?
Ngai no makasi te	I feel powerless
Navandi kaka ngai komuana mawa	I'm just sitting, hoping
Sekobanzaka yo butu moyi he	Thinking of you night and day
Zonga ko	Come back
Nasala boni	What should I do?
Nasuka wapi	Where should I go?

Instruments return; lyrics spoken in rhythm

Text repeated several times

Ngai se kolelaka	I'm crying for this love
Nga sekobanzaka yo	Thinking of you

These lyrics add an emotional layer that Dolly's original only suggested. They are less ambiguous—"I feel powerless"—and they embody the hopelessness more strongly: "it's so painful to lose what your heart loves the most" . . . "what should I do" . . . "where should I go"?

After this section, the song repeats verse 1 about Jolene's beauty rather than continuing with verse 3 (3:33). This omitted verse is where Dolly's original narrator laid it on the line to Jolene: "my happiness depends on you and whatever you decide to do." Without verse 3, and with the added lyrics of the new section, the vibe of the song changes significantly since there is less ambiguity. In this version, Jolene has already taken the narrator's man ("come back"), and the singer is bereft. The song concludes with two more choruses (3:54) before Bakalanga repeats the first line of the chorus in a free rhythm (4:41) in the same manner as the intro of the song. However, it is now clear that the line "please don't take my man" is sung in vain.

GLORIA ANN TAYLOR

While Lil Nas X did not have to change the lyrics of "Jolene" to sing it as a gay, Black man, Gloria Ann Taylor, a Black funk, soul, and R&B singer, rewrote a couple of the song's most recognizable lines to represent her identity more accurately. Taylor released the first known cover of "Jolene" in 1973. She, along with her husband and producer Walter Whisenhunt, recorded three hits that appeared on the R&B chart between 1969 and 1974, and she was nominated for a Grammy Award for Best Female R&B Vocal Performance in 1969. Taylor eventually left her music career, but in 2015 several of her recordings were reissued, and "Jolene" appears on the CD *Love Is a Hurtin' Thing* (figure 5.4). (Listen to example 5.7 ▶.)

There are several sections during her cover where the band plays funk grooves without Taylor. After the song's intro, when the vocalist usually enters on the chorus, the band continues, playing the chord changes of the full chorus. During the last couple of bars, Taylor then enters vocalizing wordlessly. Only after this longer instrumental opening does she sing the first chorus (0:32). Taylor then stakes her claim to the song in the first verse, rewriting the lyrics: "Your beauty is beyond compare with long, dark, and wavy hair, golden skin and eyes of emerald green"

FIGURE 5.4 Cover of Gloria Ann Taylor's album *Love Is a Hurtin' Thing* (2015). Photo circa 1967. Courtesy of Ubiquity Records on behalf of Leonard Taylor.

(0:53). With this small, but significant change, Taylor opens the door to a new vision of Jolene's beauty.

The band has a bigger role to play in this version compared to others: for the second chorus, Taylor only sings the first two lines without the usual phrase extension (1:36); the band then finishes that chorus and extends their playing into a repeat of the chorus, though the vibe is improvisatory—the phrase lengths do not follow the typical pattern, so the chord changes do not occur when expected. Taylor re-enters singing the third verse (2:06), and in the next chorus, she vocalizes on "Jolene," abandoning any attempt to sing the chorus straight through (2:28). Instead, layers of voices trade off singing "Jolene" and "please don't take my man," and the desperation and edge in her voice, along with the pitch, rise for the second half of the chorus, "Jolene" and "please don't take him even though you can." She then repeats the third verse, but with the lines reversed (2:50). In this chorus and the repeat of the third verse, she is riffing on the song, piecing together lines and rhythmically stretching and compressing the melody, and this improvisatory feeling continues as she repeats the chorus as before. The song's end is signaled when the vocal layers begin to fade out (3:12–3:19). But then, even as the volume continues to diminish, she comes back for more, singing "Jolene" higher and higher (3:24). While her performance does not seem as unbalanced and frenzied as The White Stripes's, it is harrowing (and thrilling) to hear her spin out at the end as she pleads with Jolene. To me, she sounds vocally and emotionally courageous.

CHIQUIS RIVERA AND BECKY G

Chiquis Rivera, a Regional Mexican music singer, and Becky G, a performer of Regional Mexican music, hip-hop, and reggaeton pop, recorded a cover in 2020 that gives "Jolene," a "brassy, cumbia swing."[15] (Listen to example 5.8 ▶.) More specifically, the style is *cumbia norteña*, which is popular in northern Mexico and the US Southwest. With one brief exception, the signature *cumbia* rhythm is present throughout the song: ♩ ♪ ♪ (a long short-short rhythm, 1 2&, with beat 2 emphasized).

The Spanish lyrics do not stray far from Dolly's.[16] But in verse 1 there are a couple of notable differences in Jolene's physical characteristics.

Spanish	**Translation**	**Original lyrics**
¡Cómo tu belleza no hay igual!	How your beauty has no equal!	Your beauty is beyond compare
Tu pelo brilla al caminar	Your hair shines when you walk	With flaming locks of auburn hair
Tus ojos verdes saben seducer	Your green eyes know how to seduce	With ivory skin and eyes of emerald green
Sonríes como la primavera	You smile like the spring	Your smile is like a breath of spring
Tu voz el canto de sirena	Your voice the siren's song	Your voice is soft like summer rain
No puedo competir contigo, Jolene	I can't compete with you, Jolene	And I cannot compete with you, Jolene

Jolene's whiteness ("ivory skin") is eliminated, and her hair color is not specified. These changes invite a wider range of racial and ethnic identities for Jolene. Not only that, but this Jolene is a seducer and a siren. In Dolly's version, one could imagine that Jolene does not necessarily seek the attention of the man who is attracted to her beauty. But now her eyes are not just green emeralds; they also seduce. And her voice is not "soft" but is that of a siren.

Another distinctive aspect of this cover is that the two singers, Chiquis and Becky G, are not set up as two different characters; neither is the narrator or Jolene. The song begins with a spoken line by Chiquis, "Si hay tantos hombres en el mundo, ¿Por qué quieres el mío?" (If there are so many men in the world, why do you want mine?). Becky G replies, "Jolene." Since there is only one speaker in the song (remember, Jolene never speaks), Chiquis and Becky G trade off singing the lead and the harmony in the verses. They share lines in the chorus and sing in unison in the middle chorus. So, their roles are equal; both are the wronged woman.

One of the features of *cumbia norteña* is the inclusion of the accordion, which is ever-present in this recording of "Jolene," playing energetic, fast figurations in the background. The recording also replaces the iconic guitar riff of Dolly's original with a quartet of trombones (the inclusion of brass is an element from *ranchera*). While the trombones do not play the polyphony (that originally existed between the bass, back beat, and melody) of Dolly's original intro, this brass opening echoes the asymmetric cross-rhythm Dolly used. The trombones also achieve the nervous energy of the guitar lick by coming in one at a time, stacking up chords that rock in parallel stepwise motion between notes, reminiscent of Dolly's opening. As the pitch rises with the addition of each new chord tone, so does the tension, which peaks at the fourth chord when the highest trombone line comes in on the 7th of the chord, rather than the tonic (example 5.1). The intro is the only place they enter one at a time; once the song begins, they always play simultaneously.

These oscillating chords on trombone are not played as often as the guitar riff was in the original, where that lick filled in after almost every line. The trombones never play during the verses, keeping the intensity lower than in the choruses. Their presence or absence plays a big part in

EXAMPLE 5.1 Chiquis and Becky G, "Jolene" (2020), trombones in intro.

manipulating the energy of the song. That is particularly noticeable in the bridge (2:18) when the two singers shout "¡cumbia!," freely improvise, and offer shout-outs to each other and to Dolly, which is a move typical in *cumbia*. The reappearance there of the trombones (after they had sat out for the previous verse) supports the exuberant vibe of the bridge. Then, once the final chorus begins, the trombones disappear as the overall texture thins to its most minimal in the song (2:45). The characteristic *cumbia* rhythm drops out and is replaced by handclaps. But after the first two lines of the chorus, the trombones return, the texture thickens again, the *cumbia* rhythm returns, and the intensity ratchets up only to stop short before the last words of the final line ("robarme el amor"/"steal my love"), which are sung a cappella in a slow, free rhythm by both performers. The trombones re-enter to play a smooth cadential riff to end the song.

The bridge between the third verse and the final chorus is a notable change to the song's structure. There the two singers vocalize freely: Chiquis gives a shout-out to "Becky G in the house; let's get it girl!" in English. Becky G replies in Spanish "¡Dile, Chiquis!" ("tell them, Chiquis!"). After both shout "¡cumbia!" Chiquis calls out, "Dolly, we love you!" and Becky G agrees, "Te queremo'." This bridge is a fun salute to the performers and Dolly, but it also serves a dramatic purpose in the music video that accompanies the song.

THE MUSIC VIDEO

The music video opens with the look of a Western film, but one straight out of pulp fiction–style comic books and B-rated action films, with the two women as heroes. (View example 5.9 ▶.) They appear in an environmental blend of live action, motion graphics, and animated imagery, overlaid with the dot pattern reminiscent of half-tone printing processes used in comics, photography, and newsprint.

The opening credits explain the setup: an "Outlaw Biker Rolling through State, a Pyromaniac Girl with a Bad Temper, and a Bounty Hunter Fell for Each Other." Chiquis is the biker and Becky G is the pyromaniac. The triangle is complicated (who exactly "fell for each other"?). This exposition of characters is set to the trombone intro. As in the song's arrangement, the two women are not cast in specific roles as the betrayed woman and the Jolene character, but are equally empowered in their black leather, silver chains, and weaponry. Throughout the video, scenes of Chiquis and Becky G singing to camera are intercut with animated action scenes of the women and the handsome bounty hunter.

At the first chorus, the action begins. We see the trio in a car chase with police; the man drives while the women do the shooting. Next, the trio robs a man in a casino. They open fire, steal his briefcase full of money, and escape to celebrate in a motel. Soon, a group of armed men arrive looking menacing. Presumably they are there to recover the stolen money, and the bounty hunter goes out to meet them. As the men talk, Chiquis and Becky G watch from their motel window. When the men pull their guns on the bounty hunter, he points to the room where the two women are. It is unclear whether he tells these guys that the money is in the room, or if he betrays the women by offering them up as payment instead of the cash. Either way, his ploy works, and he leaves as the men walk to the motel room. A knowing look passes between the two women, who then open fire on the men as they crash into the room. The bounty hunter drives away smiling as we see the gunfire flashes in the motel room.

Two weeks later, we see the bounty hunter in a diner looking into the glowing briefcase filled with money. Suddenly he is knocked over by a gun butt by someone outside the frame. He lies dazed and bleeding on the floor. This is followed by a cut to an outdoor scene. The bounty hunter is tied to a cactus, and we see his attackers: Chiquis, who holds a gasoline can, and Becky G, with a lit cigarette lighter. Both are holding guns. They toss the lighter into the open briefcase in front of the bounty hunter, who screams as the money goes up in flames. The video ends with an image of the trio: the bounty hunter is in the center, still tied to the cactus, framed by the two women in the foreground. The final line of the song ("robarme el amor") is accompanied by a shot of the two women singing, and the video closes with them posing together as classic triumphant superheroes (figure 5.5).

The video does not make narrative connections between sections of the song and scenes in the story. But the inserted bridge is aligned specifically with the pivotal moments in

FIGURE 5.5 Chiquis and Becky G, "Jolene," music video, final shot.

the video. That section (2:24) begins in the motel room as Chiquis and Becky G look at each other and plot to fight back against the intruders. The bridge continues through the gunfire and the later scene in the diner when they attack and capture the bounty hunter. The final chorus returns with the bounty hunter tied to the cactus.

The party atmosphere of the bridge—improvised lines, shout-outs, and ululations—makes the scenes of the women fighting back feel celebratory and confirms that this cover is about the alliance between the two women. The song's lyrics may suggest they are rivals for the man's attention. The video, however, is about women who refuse to be the victims of men rather than fighting over the same man. This notion was hinted at early in the video when Chiquis and Becky G, wielding swords, are shown protecting a young woman on the ground in an alleyway from a gang of men in hoodies (0:25). Any competition for the bounty hunter the two women may have felt quickly disappears when he betrays them both at the motel. At the height of the gun battle, the women call each other by name in solidarity: “Becky G in the house,” “Let’s get it girl!” and “¡Dile Chiquis!” The name Jolene is superimposed over the women’s superhero photo at the end of the video. The explosion in the background of that image suggests the fiery nature of these two women, both of whom have all of Jolene’s power as well as the betrayed woman’s refusal now to be a victim.

HEARING FROM DOLLY, CHIQUIS, AND BECKY G

For the Latin Recording Academy’s *Essal y su música* special in 2021, Dolly joined Chiquis in a virtual duet in a performance of “Jolene.” (View example 5.10 ▶.) From her remote studio, Dolly said:

> *Buenas noches*, y’all! I would never pass up the opportunity to celebrate women in music in any language. We owe it to ourselves to stick together and lift each other up. Sometimes that means having courage to have hard and honest conversations about the things that matter most. Now these icons of Regional Mexican music have set their courage to song from cumbia to ranchera and mariachi: here are Aída Cuevas and kicking it off with one of my personal favorite hearts-to-hearts songs, *mi amiga* Chiquis![17]

Dolly’s remarks echo the message of this cover of “Jolene,” in which the women “stick together and lift each other up.”

Chiquis had this to say about performing the song. “Dolly is an icon in music and for women. . . . It is an honor to sing this song in Spanish.” Becky G commented, “I was fascinated by the idea because it brings together our two worlds. When they ask me where I am from, I always say that I am Mexican. I never say that my grandparents are Mexican and I am American. However, country music was always heard in my house, with the Mexican, and our 'Jolene' is that. It has the essence of Dolly with a little bit of our itch."[18]

Chiquis and Becky G's video interpretation of "Jolene" seems as much an answer song as a cover since it significantly alters the script of Dolly's original. In their performance and in the music video, Chiquis and Becky G seem to be floating above the song, offering a new way to imagine the relationship between the song's narrator and Jolene. As we will see in the next chapter, many "Jolene" answer songs are from Jolene's perspective. She finally gets a voice in the women's encounter about a man. But in this performance, the women opt out of the rival scenario altogether and create a new story about female comradery and solidarity.

PART III

ANSWER SONGS TO "JOLENE"

CHAPTER 6

JOLENE SPEAKS

"JOLENE" IS A SONG that begs for an answer: "my happiness depends on you and whatever you decide to do, Jolene." So it is no surprise that several artists have recorded answer songs, most of which spring from the desire to hear directly from Jolene.

Answer songs were especially popular in country music in the 1950s, 1960s, and 1970s. The most famous is Kitty Wells's recording "It Wasn't God Who Made Honky Tonk Angels." Written by J. D. Miller, the song responds to Hank Thompson's 1952 recording "The Wild Side of Life," in which a man scolds his wife for preferring honky tonk nightlife to homelife: "I didn't know God made honky tonk angels, I might have known you'd never make a wife." Wells's reply

Dolly Parton's Jolene. Lydia R. Hamessley, Oxford University Press. © Oxford University Press 2025.
DOI: 10.1093/9780197760345.003.0007

pushes back: "Too many times married men think they're still single that has caused many a good girl to go wrong. It's a shame that all the blame is on us women." Answer songs like this example typically used the same melody and often reused original lyrics along with new ones to offer a different perspective on the situation.

The songs that reply to "Jolene," however, are newly written and from Jolene's viewpoint, but with different approaches. In some Jolene is a willing participant in the affair, while in others she has been deceived by the man and does not want to continue the relationship. In one example, both women sing about the scenario from their different perspectives, and their feelings are remarkably similar.

WHITE RABBIT OBJECT, "JOLENE'S REPLY"; KIRSTY MACCOLL, "CAROLINE"

In "Jolene's Reply" (2020) by the band wht.rbbt.obj (White Rabbit Object), Jolene takes a "sorry, not sorry" stance that paints her character just as badly as we feared (Listen to example 6.1 ▶.)

> Sorry that I give him the type of love that's so full grown
> Sorry that I give it to him in ways you can't understand
> But honey I'm not sorry that I took your man

The sound of this alternative rock band matches the vibe of Jolene's "who cares," snotty attitude. As Greg Kot of NPR said, "This song swings like a wrecking ball . . . Heavily distorted roadhouse raunch . . . The dirtiest groove I've heard in a long time."[1] The band explained their reason for writing "Jolene's Reply": "It seemed everyone was singing about this gal that stole Dolly Parton's man. We thought it was high time that Jolene had a voice in the matter." They were right, there had been earlier "Jolene" answer songs. But most give Jolene a conscience, and she regrets her role as homewrecker.

Like "Jolene's Reply," the Jolene character in Kirsty MacColl's song "Caroline" (1995) remains in the relationship with the man. (Listen to example 6.2 ▶.) However, she feels guilty about it, especially since she is the best friend of Caroline, the betrayed woman.

> How could you walk out on her and turn to her best friend
> It was wrong from the start I wish I'd turned you away
> And my head said go, but my heart, my heart said stay
> And now I don't want to see Caroline

MacColl explained her response to "Jolene," which she thought of as a victim song: "A lot of the songs I heard growing up were written by men for women. There was a lot of, 'Oh, I can't live without my man.' I don't write songs about women as victims. I think it's been done to death."[2]

JENNIFER NETTLES, "THAT GIRL"; CAM, "DIANE"

Two other answer songs take a different approach. In them, Jolene is unhappy being the other woman and mortified at finding herself in that position. Victimhood is not absent in these songs, though it is not clear whether the victim is the cheated-on spouse, the other woman, or both. In each song, the Jolene character is just as deceived by the man as his partner and is stunned to find out that he is already married (or in a relationship).

Nettles said "That Girl" (2013) was inspired by the ambiguity of Dolly's original: "All we hear from Dolly is her one perspective as the narrator. But what if Jolene doesn't want to take her man just because she can? We never know."[3] (View and listen to examples 6.3a and 6.3b ▶.) In the song, Nettles's character calls the woman to tip her off about her cheating lover: "See I always kind of liked you, so, I wanna have your back." She does not want to hurt another woman, and she does not want the "dirty looks" that will come her way as the other woman. She also names the specter of Jolene in her song: "Imagine how surprised I was when he got up to leave. It wasn't my name on his lips. No, he didn't call for me. He didn't say, Jolene." Nettles told her co-writer, Butch Walker, that the song "should really be called 'The Ballad of Jolene' in parentheses."[4]

Nettles's song, like Dolly's, is in a minor mode. But rather than having an ancient or folky sound like "Jolene," "That Girl" has a contemporary vibe through the energetic percussion of handclaps, congas, and a "faux Latin groove."[5] Its melodically repetitive chorus captures the characters' insistence that she does not want to be "that girl." This chorus is as single-minded and unrelenting as Dolly's with her four-part reiteration of Jolene's name. Only now it is the Jolene character who begs to be heard.

In Cam's "Diane" (2017), the Jolene character also reaches out to the wife, Diane, pleading with her to believe that "I didn't know he was your man." (View and listen to examples 6.4a and 6.4b ▶.) It is important to her that Diane understand the situation. As Cam said about the song, “It’s the apology so many spouses deserve, but never get.”[6] Cam’s recording is insistent, upbeat, almost frantic, and in a major mode. The song begins with an a cappella chorus—a wall of sound, sung with pitch correction and reverb that reinforces the singer’s insistent plea:

> Oh, I promise I didn’t know he was your man
> I would’ve noticed a gold wedding band, Diane
> I’d rather you hate me than not understand
> Oh, Diane

Cam (like MacColl in “Caroline”) names the jilted spouse in the song’s chorus. In their songs, the other woman pleads with the betrayed partner, addressing her over and over by name in the chorus, and titling the song with her name. This move inverts Dolly’s “Jolene,” which repeats the other woman’s name.

The runaway pacing of “Diane,” combined with the strident harmony of the chorus, suggests a desperation in the singer’s appeal to Diane, as in Nettles’s “That Girl.” In both songs, the singer seems panicked as she speaks to the betrayed woman. However, in “Diane,” the insistent, galloping percussion captures the Jolene character’s frenzied and agitated desire to assuage her guilt more than it portrays her remorse and sadness in being betrayed herself. Some critics hear the song’s arrangement as “too frantic and upbeat for the words Cam is saying,” and that “the multi-layered harmonics feel like a machination of digital studio manipulations instead of the inspiring results of hiring an actual 4-piece singing quartet to capture the chorus in a live setting.”[7]

The high energy and fast pacing of "Diane" made it ripe for a version by Sister Sadie, an all-woman bluegrass band. (Listen to example 6.5 ▶.) However, in their setting, the singer does not feel as desperate and on edge as in Cam's recording, which moves along at 142 bpm, compared to Sister Sadie's at 128–132 bpm. The slower, less agitated pace, along with the very human three-part bluegrass harmony, the absence of percussion, and the presence of the fiddle, creates a less frenetic, more warm tone.

Like Dolly's original, these answer songs—"Caroline," "That Girl," and "Diane"—focus on the dynamic between the two women. However, in the latter two songs, the Jolene character wants to tell the truth about the situation directly to the woman who is cheated on by her husband or lover. She seeks to protect and empower the betrayed woman. An alliance between the women, rather than competition, is possible in these songs, and the underlying message is that the guy is not worth the pain he has caused for either of them.

> I know boys can be promiscuous, yeah, that's just what they do
> But this involves the both of us, yeah, it's our business too
> . . .
> I'm calling 'cause I really thought you should know
> Even though he's being that guy
> I don't want to be that girl with your guy
>
> —"That Girl," Nettles

> Believing the words that he said
> How could we be such fools?
> And all those nights that he's given to me

I wish that I could give them back to you
. . .
But you're only cheating yourself
Choosing him over the truth
—"Diane," Cam

Cam said she did not want her song "to be angry or about slut-shaming or bashing other women. I wanted it to be empowering, like people sticking together by telling the truth and having that integrity."[8]

CARLY PEARCE AND ASHLEY MCBRYDE, "NEVER WANTED TO BE THAT GIRL"

While we hear directly from the other woman in "Jolene's Reply," "Caroline, "That Girl," and "Diane," in Carly Pearce and Ashley McBryde's "Never Wanted to Be That Girl" (2021), both women in the triangle speak. (View and listen to examples 6.6a and 6.6b ▶.) In the first verse, McBryde sings the part of the other women who is mortified when she realizes she is in a relationship with a married man:

What started out as one night turned to six months just like that
He never had a ring on so I never thought to ask
But then last night I saw a message on his phone
That said, "Hey, babe, what time you comin' home?"

The chorus, sung by McBryde in the lead with Pearce on harmony, focuses on the singer's feelings about being the other woman.

I never wanted to be that girl
I never wanted to hate myself

I thought this kind of lonely only happens to somebody else
Bein' the other one when there's another one
God, this feels like hell

In the second verse, we now hear from Pearce as the cheated-on wife, with McBryde singing harmony:

I heard about those women who didn't have a clue
The ones that made excuses like my mama used to do
And he jumps in the shower just as soon as he gets home
And I spend half an hour goin' through his phone

Then when the chorus comes back, word for word, with Pearce carrying the lead, the women are united in their shared misery, filled with anguish and despair, not guilt or blame. In the song's bridge, their feelings are expressed with alternating lines that apply to both women.

Wife: Oh, and I feel stupid
Lover: I feel cheap
Wife: I feel used
Lover: I feel weak

Like Dolly's "Jolene" (and unlike "That Girl" and "Diane"), Pearce and McBryde do not "call the guy a crapsack," in McBryde's words. She explained, "There's so many times we fight over each other and blame each other, and I think what's interesting is each woman's realization: 'Oh my goodness, I never thought I would find myself in this scenario.' "[9]

These "Jolene" answer songs feel as though they are sung in the heat of the moment: the realization of betrayal is fresh, and the responses are immediate. But an answer song by Chapel Hart gives the cheated-on partner some time to think things over. The response is dramatically different: "you can have him Jolene."

7

"YOU CAN HAVE HIM JOLENE"

"YOU CAN HAVE HIM Jolene" by Chapel Hart was inspired by a T-shirt (figure 7.1). In my interview with the group—a trio of African American women, sisters Danica and Devynn Hart and their cousin Trea Swindle—they told me they were filming a music video for their cover of Dolly's "9 to 5," acting as workers in a diner, when Devynn showed up wearing a T-shirt that said, "YOU CAN HAVE HIM [signed]—Jolene." (View example 7.1 ▶.) Danica, the lead singer, immediately thought, "How is she gonna take something of mine and tell me I can have him back? You know what, matter of fact, *you* can have him Jolene. We ain't got to fight over him."[1] Chapel Hart decided he was just not worth the bother, and their song flips the Jolene story.

Dolly Parton's Jolene. Lydia R. Hamessley, Oxford University Press. © Oxford University Press 2025.
DOI: 10.1093/9780197760345.003.0008

FIGURE 7.1 Chapel Hart, T-shirt in "9 to 5" music video.

The trio is named for the Harts Chapel community in their hometown of Poplarville, Mississippi (figure 7.2). Soon after they wrote "You Can Have Him Jolene," they sang it for Leslie Fram, senior vice president of music strategy for Country Music Television (CMT), which inducted the group into the Next Women of Country for 2021. The trio reports that when Fram heard the song, she said, "'Chapel Hart, in fifty years of country music, no one has ever said this,' . . . and 'this song is going to be massive.'" (Listen to example 7.2 ▶.) Danica explained their new take on Dolly's song: "I don't know in 1974 if you could have said, 'you know what, I know that you're cheating, that you're messing with my man, and guess what, you can have him.'"

As Fram predicted, the song catapulted the group onto the national scene. "You Can Have Him Jolene," from their second album *The Girls Are Back in Town* (2021), went to number four on the *Billboard* Country Digital Song Sales Chart in 2021. The song found an even wider audience

FIGURE 7.2 Chapel Hart, l. to r. Trea Swindle, Danica Hart, and Devynn Hart. Courtesy of Chapel Hart; photo by Saddi Edwards.

in the summer of 2022 when the trio performed it on the seventeenth season of *America's Got Talent* (AGT). The show's judges rewarded their stellar performance with a rare Golden Buzzer, which guaranteed the group a spot in the finals. Although the trio came in fifth, "You Can Have Him Jolene" garnered a lot of praise, including from Dolly who tweeted, "What a fun new take on my song, @ ChapelHartBand!"[2]

A few days after the AGT finals in September 2022, they sang the song at their debut on the Grand Ole Opry. Devynn said that AGT gave them "opportunities that we didn't think were possible." Danica chimed in, "It's changed everything, but we ain't done yet."[3] They recorded another album, continued to tour widely, and made more appearances on the Opry. They are especially committed to their fans on social media and in person, spending hours talking with and hugging people who drive many miles to see them.

The group performed at the CMT Awards show in April 2023, and in an interview there Danica said:

> we're showing and representing that Black people have lived and have the country experience too. And I think that for so long it's just only looked one certain type of way. . . . We are so proud. And I think that for so long we were just in the grind, so we didn't even pay attention to like, we're Black women making strides in country. We're just like: work, work, work, work, work.

Trea added, "There isn't a better time and place than right now for us to be where we are in the music industry. And not even just African American. Of all body sizes, body types."[4]

"You Can Have Him Jolene" appeared in the midst of country music's reckoning with the acceptance of Black artists in the early 2020s. Along with the work and advocacy of Black Opry and Color Me Country Radio, to name but two, Chapel Hart's presence and huge success was another indication that things might be changing. According to Trea, "There are still so many barriers that need to come down. I'm just proud that we get to play a role in knocking those down. Let us be that sledgehammer."[5]

THE SONG

When Danica first saw that T-shirt, her reaction was, "there's no way we're still fighting over the same man from

1974. How do we go back and tell this story for right now? How do we go back and tell her that she can have him? And I remember writing down the line 'well since the last song I've had time to think it over,' and then it was like, 'a lot of tears, a lot of beer, a lot of wine.' And it just seemed like the floodgate kind of opened up for the story to really write itself." With those two lines, the song launches us into the story. The singer has agonized about her cheating partner, fought and made up with him countless times, finally stopped thinking things will get better, and left him. She then finds a man who loves and respects her.

"You Can Have Him Jolene," simultaneously lighthearted and threatening, is a rousing country-rock song filled with sass. The prominent electric guitar kicks off the song with a freight-train pulse accompanied by electronic sound effects. The piano and steel guitar round out the country-rock sound. The band pulls out all the stops for a rocking guitar solo in the instrumental verse between choruses near the end of the song. The trio of vocalists is led by Danica in the verses. In the chorus, all three sing their lines in such tight harmony that it is hard to tell which line is the melody—an appealing sonic embodiment of their sisterly solidarity.[6]

The fun lies in the chorus when the singer takes control with the zinger "you can have him Jolene."

> Oh Jolene, you can have him 'cause he don't mean much to me
> Well, I cried so much 'til rivers turned to seas
> Oh Jolene, when you think that he's in love, he'll surely leave
> Like he did me
> You can have him, Jolene

Unlike in Dolly's song, Jolene's name is not repeated in endless pleading. Instead, the piling up of the long E sound (Jolene, he, me, seas, Jolene, he's, he'll, leave) feels assertive. Also, in the final chorus, the last line is sung three times. The first two times end with a deceptive cadence (on a minor vi chord), and the final time the rhythm is stretched out before closing on the tonic chord. Both gestures hammer home the point to Jolene.

On first listen, "You Can Have Him Jolene" seems like a straightforward verse/chorus song (figure 7.3). But a closer look reveals some touches of formal, textual, and musical inspiration that enhance the song's message. The song seems to have three verses, each four phrases long, with choruses interspersed, and an instrumental verse before the final chorus. However, the opening section is musically different enough from the other verses that it functions as an intro rather than a verse. The first two phrases of the intro do not return at the beginnings of the subsequent verses. Moreover, the harmony of this intro is static in comparison

Intro Verse
    abcd'
Verse 1
    efcd
Chorus
Verse 2
    efad
Chorus
Instrumental Verse
Chorus

FIGURE 7.3. "You Can Have Him Jolene" outline of form. Each of the musical phrases of the verses is labeled with a lower-case letter. Phrase d′ ends with an open-ended cadence on the third scale degree of the tonic chord. Phrase d ends with a fully closed cadence on the first scale degree of the tonic chord.

to the other two verses. This slower harmonic rhythm underpins the opening lyrics that point to the backstory of the song, Dolly's "Jolene."

Danica explained they opened their song with this line—"well since the last song I've had time to think it over"—because they figured some younger listeners might not know Dolly's original.

> I wanted to find a way to tie the bigness of Jolene. . . . I didn't want to bypass "Jolene" that Dolly had written. . . . If you really try to get into it and tell the backstory we're gonna miss so much of [our own] song. But I figured with that line, if you never heard "Jolene" before, you gotta go, "well since the last song? How does this work?"

Trea suggested that first line is "like a bridge to a new generation," with Danica chiming in, "Now you gotta go do the homework. That's the setup, but we were able to get on with just telling the story in today's time." She added, "It's the one line that if you wanna really know the story you gotta go pay attention to this line, and you gotta go back and get it for yourself, and you tie the worlds together."

The melody of that important opening line starts on the upper tonic and moves stepwise down the scale, harmonized by an A chord until the half cadence in an E chord at the end of the second line. The E-major sonority continues through the third and fourth phrases, which melodically circle around the lower notes of the scale. The intro ends with a cadence back on A, but with the melody on the third of the chord. So, although the intro returns to the tonic, it feels open-ended. After all, this section introduces the story, which continues immediately in the next verses. Starting the song in the upper octave with that strong melodic gesture, static harmonic rhythm, and open-ended cadence, coupled with the reference to "the last song," immediately hooks the listener.

Conversely, verses 1 and 2 start in the lower register and are set to a quicker harmonic rhythm as the details of the contemporary story pour out. Phrases 3 and 4 of these verses loosely reprise the melody of phrases 3 and 4 of the intro verse, but differently harmonized, and both verses end with a fully closed cadence with the melody on the tonic, instead of the open-ended cadence of the intro verse.

However, there is one significant difference between verses 1 and 2 that occurs in verse 2 with the third line: "well I found a man who loves me and he'll give me all I need" (1:27). Rather than repeating the melody of the third line from verse 1, the melody of that line in verse 2 reprises a variant of the opening melody of the intro verse: the scalewise descent from the upper octave (example 7.1). Listeners might not recognize the repetition of the opening line since it is harmonized differently. In the intro, the line was sung over the tonic chord (A); here in verse 2 the line is sung over the sub-dominant chord (D), which resolves to the tonic chord on the word *give*.

This line is also textually distinctive. Most lines in each verse (including most of the intro verse) feature internal rhymes. But the third line of the verse 2—which brings back the opening melody—has no internal rhymes. Trea explained that the internal rhymes were not useful for that pivotal line in verse 2: "It's direct. Don't get lost in the song

EXAMPLE 7.1 Chapel Hart, "You Can Have Him Jolene" (2021).

(a) Intro verse, line 1.

(b) Verse 2, line 3.

and the fancy wordplay. Like you need to take this home." There were also no internal rhymes in the first line of the intro verse. Thus, the two lines—"well since the last song I've had time to think it over" and "I found a man who loves me and he'll give me all I need"—are linked textually as well as melodically.

This line from verse 2 is the crux of the song's message. According to Danica, "it's a big line. You'll never be able to know what you can have if you don't let go of what you got. If you don't let go of what's not serving you, you don't know if you can get anything greater. The greater may not be getting another man. It may be, 'I didn't know I liked to go out and listen to live music. I didn't know I like to stay up and eat ice cream and watch scary movies,' 'cause you've been living for . . . to hold onto this thing for so long."

In Trea's view, when Dolly wrote "Jolene," "it was still very much a 'Stand by Your Man' era. It doesn't matter if he drinks or if he beats you, if he does all the things, you still gotta deal with it. . . . And I kind of feel like that might have been what Dolly wanted to say ['you can have him'], but being in that time, you have to do it in a way that was accepted at the time. . . . Back in the day, once you were married that was it, and if he stepped out, you just had to work it out. . . . This ain't back in the day."

In fact, when the trio released the song as a single, it was accompanied by a photo mashup of the women in a retro kitchen, appealing to the notion that the original "Jolene" was "back in the day" (figure 7.4). As Danica said about the photo, "You can have him, and we'll bring over food for the celebration, OK?"

FIGURE 7.4 Chapel Hart, "You Can Have Him Jolene" single, cover art. Courtesy of Chapel Hart.

But despite the retro era vibe they ascribed to Dolly's original, the trio also saw Dolly as being gutsy and assertive in "Jolene." Danica said, "this is how it played out in my brain: [Dolly] got out there and said, 'oh, she *is* cute. I understand why he went after you with your beautiful green eyes, red hair. But listen, I'm just telling you, I know about you, and this is your warning.' So, it's not that she's weak, even though a lot of people hear it that way. It takes a lot of woman to stand up and go, 'listen, look, I love him and I got a lot invested here, so I'm asking you to let him go.' "

Devynn suggested that their song is truer to "this generation of women [who] are just a little bit spicier, and a little bit sassier. And I think in this day and age, things like Jolene do happen, but I think the approach that a lot of women take are completely different nowadays." Trea added that part of the power of Dolly's song (and theirs) is in simply naming the problem: "As long as it's secret, it's alright. But once the cover's been pulled off. . . ."

Indeed, it is a powerful move to uncover the full situation in the song and address everyone involved. While Dolly's song can be heard as assertive because she directly confronts Jolene, in "You Can Have Him Jolene," the wronged partner airs the affair, its effects, and its aftermath for all to hear, not just Jolene. Trea explained: "if you look at [our song] in contrast to 'Jolene,' . . . the reality of the situation is that 'it's not just me and you honey, it's me, you *and* him. We *all* gotta talk about it.' " This is why they address the man in their song. According to Trea, "He's part of it too. Why don't I let him know, like 'you're the problem, and you're gonna have the problem now.' "

Thus, in the intro verse, the singer addresses the listener directly, telling us about her situation and to remember "the last song." Then in verse 1, the singer shifts and speaks directly to her cheating man in lines 1 and 2 ("you holdin' me and sayin' you were wrong"), and in line 4, the singer talks to directly Jolene ("he's your problem"). Verse 2 again addresses the listener and, presumably, Jolene. The chorus is fully aimed at Jolene, though we, as listeners, also "hear" the lines as the betrayed woman goes public with her story. Trea described their approach: it is "almost like an open letter to not just yourself but everybody in the whole situation because, it's like putting it all on the table."

The trio carefully crafted these shifts. Danica added that the song "takes you on a journey. Like if you were gonna write it out . . ., but as you're writing, the story becomes more real again. . . . To address the person in the moment in the story kinda brings it back to where you can like see the fight between the two. I can see her now telling Jolene like, 'look he's your problem. If you think you've got him, go ahead girl.' "

THE MUSIC VIDEO

While the trio sings about the problem in their song, in the music video they show us just how much of a problem this guy is going to have. (View example 7.3 ▶.) In it we see the wronged woman (played by Danica), the cheating lover, and Jolene duke it out in a bar fight (with Danica aided by Devynn and Trea). It is raucous fun. The video opens with a twenty-one-second tour of a "small QUIET town in South Mississippi." Only ambient sound accompanies idyllic views of the area, then a fade to black. The tranquility of the small-town setting is suddenly shattered when the electric guitar kicks off the song. Here comes trouble.

During the intro verse, we see Danica in bed trying to sleep while her partner checks his text messages from Jolene. At the start of verse 1, he leaves the room, and she checks his phone and tries to go back to sleep. In the chorus, he returns to the bedroom and texts Jolene, arranging to meet her at the Whiskey Bar. As verse 2 begins, the scene changes to the bar where we see him and Jolene (with her long red hair). Enter Trea and Devynn who recognize him and text Danica to let her know he is cheating on her.

Ready for a fight, the trio re-enters the bar with Danica leading the way. She immediately strips off her jacket and confronts her man. Jolene pops up and gets in Danica's face, thus starting the physical fight, which plays out during the rocking instrumental verse. Danica snatches off Jolene's wig revealing her brown hair, and more people join the brawl (figure 7.5). Soon the police arrive. In the

FIGURE 7.5 Chapel Hart, "You Can Have Him Jolene" music video.

final chorus, scenes of the bar fight are intercut with the trio handcuffed and being stuffed into a police car. They are unfazed, and Danica is particularly feisty as she continues to sing "you can have him Jolene" right in a police officer's face. That last line is sung three times, and she really milks the open-endedness of the two deceptive cadences and the expanded length of the last line. The video closes to the outro music with scenes of the trio in jail and being released the next morning. They high-five one another, look around a moment, and then saunter off stage left in front of the police department building of the City of Pass Christian, Mississippi.

The video is a sing-along and dance-along romp. Its bar fight is right out of a cartoon; everything is in good fun. But amid all this hilarity, the video raises the question: why, if you are okay with letting Jolene have him, are you still fighting with her? As I started to pose that question, Devynn interrupted me: "I already know what you're going to say. Listen, listen, it's like, 'yes, you can have him, but *right* before I do that, I'm gonna give you the ass-whipping you deserve . . ., because somebody has to teach you the lesson.'" Trea added, "it's almost like, 'would you like fries with that? You can have the meal, but these are the fries.'" Danica suggested that "the video is the subconscious of what every woman really wants to do: 'if I had the chance, I would light you *up*.' So, for me, every woman who's been [cheated on], I know they watch this video and go (in the back of their mind), '*yes*!'"

When Dolly tells her own backstory of "Jolene" in concerts, she often says that Jolene snatched off Dolly's wig during their fight. So, I wondered if they had included the wig moment in their video as an homage to Dolly's story. No, they did not know that detail. Trea said its inclusion in the video was "serendipitous." Danica interpreted the video's wig snatch in a symbolic way since Jolene was revealed to not even be a real redhead:

> It was important . . . to show that "you left me for this redhead, so she'll lie about being a redhead, what else is she lying about? You left me because you were in love with a red-haired, green-eyed woman, and her hair wasn't even red! She was fake. The whole thing." [The wig snatch was] symbolism for "you thought that this is what you wanted, but it wasn't even real."

The trio also pointed out that Jolene, not Danica, starts the fight in the video. Danica explained: "I go to confront him ('what do you think that you're doing?') and [Jolene] says, 'you don't talk to him like that.' '*Girl*, who are you? Who do you think you are?'" Devynn remarked, Jolene may have started the fight, "and we just so happen to finish it." Trea added, "we came to confront her about the situation but first of all, 'miss ma'am, you're in the wrong, so why are you upset?'" Danica summed it all up by saying, "I feel like the video should be called "*Now* You Can Have Him Jolene."

Chapel Hart's rendition of the Jolene story focuses on what women can discover by letting go of the thing (in this case a man) that is not serving their wellbeing. Restoration of the betrayed woman's power is at the center of their song: she abandons the rivalry with Jolene and reclaims her life.

AFTER AGT

The day after their appearance on AGT, Loretta Lynn wrote to the trio on Facebook: "I love it, ladies. Now I'm wondering what you might be able to do with one of my songs!" Chapel Hart took up the challenge. Instead of flipping Lynn's song, "Fist City," they pick up where Lynn left off. The other woman has now been sent to Fist City, and our trio appears in the amusing song and video as the city's sheriff, mayor, and judge. (Listen to example 7.4 ▶.) (View and listen to examples 7.5a and 7.5b ▶.) They call back to "Jolene" with the lyrics, "with your eyes of emerald green and your long auburn hair, why couldn't you find your own southern man?" They also bring back the wig: "hold onto your wig and hold onto your britches and welcome to Fist City." Chapel Hart is not in the business of writing only answer songs. But they admit that "so much of our music is inspired by the artists that we grew up with. It's our gift of giving back, of saying thank you to the Dollys and the Patsys who have truly laid down this foundation."

"You Can Have Him Jolene" has been a life-changing song for many people. The group tells of countless times that someone has said to them, "I've been in a loveless marriage for twenty years. Thank you, this is the song I needed." The song has also been life-changing for Chapel Hart; they "had no idea the wings that this song was gonna take." After their acclaimed performance of the song on AGT, to thunderous applause and a standing ovation, Danica was in tears. (View example 7.6 ▶.) One of the judges, Simon Cowell, asked them if they had been "trying to get a record deal or a big break." Barely able to speak, Danica explained,

"We've been trying to break into Nashville for the last couple of years. But it's been kinda hard when I think country music doesn't always look like us." Cowell replied, "You've just got to break down that door, and you may have just broken down the door with that performance, trust me."[7]

Like Cowell, some in the country music industry were predicting big things for the trio. Marcus Dowling, prominent Nashville music journalist, wrote in 2022 after their Grand Ole Opry debut, "the approachable yet exciting nature of how they perform their art separates them from previous presentations of Black performers at this level in country music. It makes them a wholly unique game changer in the genre's industry."[8]

But, as with many talented Black artists in country music, the group has faced several roadblocks. They have yet to be signed by a major label or get substantial radio play, even though they have garnered a lot of attention in the country music industry. As a result, they have shifted their goals. Danica explained their new approach a few days after they attended the 2023 Country Music Association (CMA) Awards show (where everyone knew them):

> This is to serve notice that we are no longer competing in the industry. . . . We're here to write the songs that makes you feel good from the inside out. . . . We got to get back to our original commitment. . . . We started to make people happy, to write music that people love, to watch people grow, to grow with our fans.[9]

The group will still perform, but for now they will not play ticketed shows exclusively. They will also perform for free at schools, hospitals, and other public venues.

Dowling offered an economic critique that partly explained Chapel Hart's challenges with breaking into Nashville: country music has grown "past its blue-collar fanbase" and that "uniquely impacted Chapel Hart. . . . The country artists who eventually become arena and stadium openers appeal to a different socioeconomic crowd." Trea noted, "Fans whose personal integrity is tied to what country music has historically represented probably haven't been to an arena or stadium to see a country music concert in 30 years but want to take their families to [a] smaller venue."[10]

Nonetheless, as Jon Freeman writes, the group is a conduit for bringing new fans into country music. Danica explained:

> What I've seen from "You Can Have Him Jolene" is that this generation of kids and especially children who weren't country fans by any stretch, they're going "Dang, who is this heifer Jolene and why do we not like her?" So they're having to go back to listen to Dolly's song.[11]

Chapel Hart's cover song has undoubtedly introduced new listeners to Dolly Parton and "Jolene," and it has gotten the trio a lot of attention. Unfortunately, Nashville has not opened its doors and radio stations to enough of the talented women, artists of color, and queer musicians in country music who have compelling perspectives on older hits like "Jolene" and fresh musical approaches that tell new stories across a variety of identities and life experiences.

PART IV

ENCORES OF "JOLENE"

CHAPTER 8

RETURNING TO DOLLY

Dolly took "Jolene" with her to the Rock & Roll Hall of Fame in 2022. When she learned she was included on the ballot for induction into the Hall of Fame, Dolly initially declined because she did not want to displace any rock musicians. But when she was inducted, she decided to earn her place and put together *Rockstar*. Although this album did not include "Jolene," she released a bonus track of a rock version of the song she recorded with the Italian rock band Måneskin. (Listen to example 8.1 ▶.) For her part of the Induction Ceremony concert, Dolly closed with "Jolene." (View example 8.2 ▶.)

We expect an encore at the end of a concert, usually something not yet heard. In the past, however, audiences who shouted "Encore!" wanted the performer to repeat

Dolly Parton's Jolene. Lydia R. Hamessley, Oxford University Press. © Oxford University Press 2025.
DOI: 10.1093/9780197760345.003.0009

a piece: "we want to hear it again!" Dolly has performed "Jolene" again and again, usually sticking close to her original 1974 recording. But she has also refashioned the song several times since its release fifty years ago. Dolly re-recorded "Jolene" for her album *Something Special* (1995), embraced an orchestral sound for the soundtrack for the film *Dumplin'* (2018), and dramatized "Jolene" in a Netflix television series, *Heartstrings* (2019).

SOMETHING SPECIAL

Dolly included two of her most popular songs on her thirty-third studio album, *Something Special*—"I Will Always Love You" and "Jolene"—just as both songs were on her album *Jolene*. The more successful re-release was "I Will Always Love You," performed in a duet with Vince Gill, which won the CMA award for Vocal Event of the Year. The album's producer, Steve Buckingham, called their duet "the biggie from that album," although he said he had not wanted to open the album with that song because he "knew 'I Will Always Love You' was going to be a huge record with Vince." He added, "It was so associated with her, I didn't want to start with that. I didn't want to start with 'Jolene' for the same reason."[1] So, it is at the seventh track of *Something Special* that we hear the familiar sounds of "Jolene." (Listen to example 8.3 ▶.) But we soon hear several changes: the timbre and instrumentation, some of the melodic lines, the tempo and rhythm, and the form (figure 8.1).

Dolly's new version is less folky than her original, with more influence from rock—electric guitar and drums (not the bongos of the 1974 recording). The steel guitar's presence keeps things country. Everything is bathed in reverb. This refashioning of "Jolene" begins with a shimmering cymbal and strong bass to launch the familiar acoustic guitar lick Dolly wrote in the early 1970s. As in the original, guitar lick punctuates the ends of lines, but it is now surrounded with more accompaniment from the band. Eventually, in verse 3 (and faintly in the last chorus), this riff is played on the piano instead of guitar. But the guitar reclaims its leading role in the outro. After the coda, when Dolly sings Jolene's name a couple of times, the song could have ended, echoing the original recording (3:13). Instead, an extended section built on the guitar riff takes the song out. For a full thirty seconds, the guitar's pulsing, nervous energy continues, punctuated by interjections from the electric guitar, steel guitar, and Dolly singing *Jolene* faintly.

Dolly changes the way she sings some of the melodic lines in this version. She tends to vary melodies by substituting notes or adding embellishing notes at the ends of lines. Listen, for example, to the one-note change she makes on the words "auburn" and "eyes" in the first verse (0:35). In the original, she sang a step-wise melody from the tonic to the 5th scale degree before moving back to tonic at the cadence. Here, she extends that stepwise motion by one note up to the 6th scale degree. Yes, it is a tiny change, but what a difference that one note makes in the emotional quality of the line. The added note is a brief dissonance with the chord at that point, and the momentary upward striving (only to immediately fall back to the 5th scale degree) tweaks the yearning of the lyrics. She embellishes the second lines in the verses in a similar way (on the line "summer rain," she

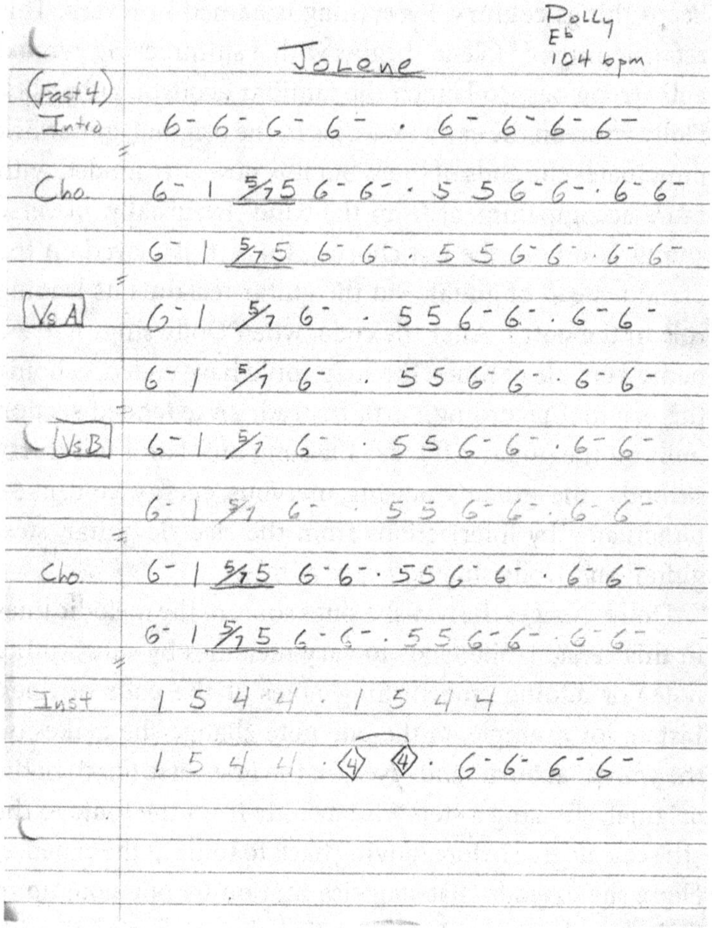

Dolly
E♭
104 bpm

Jolene

(Fast 4)

Intro 6- 6- 6- 6- · 6- 6- 6- 6-

Cho. 6- 1 5/7 5 6- 6- · 5 5 6- 6- · 6- 6-

6- 1 5/7 5 6- 6- · 5 5 6- 6- · 6- 6-

Vs A 6- 1 5/7 6- · 5 5 6- 6- · 6- 6-

6- 1 5/7 6- · 5 5 6- 6- · 6- 6-

Vs B 6- 1 5/7 6- · 5 5 6- 6- · 6- 6-

6- 1 5/7 6- · 5 5 6- 6- · 6- 6-

Cho. 6- 1 5/7 5 6- 6- · 5 5 6- 6- · 6- 6-

6- 1 5/7 5 6- 6- · 5 5 6- 6- · 6- 6-

Inst 1 5 4 4 · 1 5 4 4

1 5 4 4 · ⟨4⟩ ⟨4⟩ · 6- 6- 6- 6-

FIGURE 8.1a Dolly Parton, "Jolene," *Something Special*, 1995, studio chart by and courtesy of Steve Buckingham.

returns to the 6th scale degree, as she did on "auburn"). This new pattern returns in the remaining verses. Another way Dolly embellishes her original melody is at the ends of the verse lines, where occasionally she circles around the

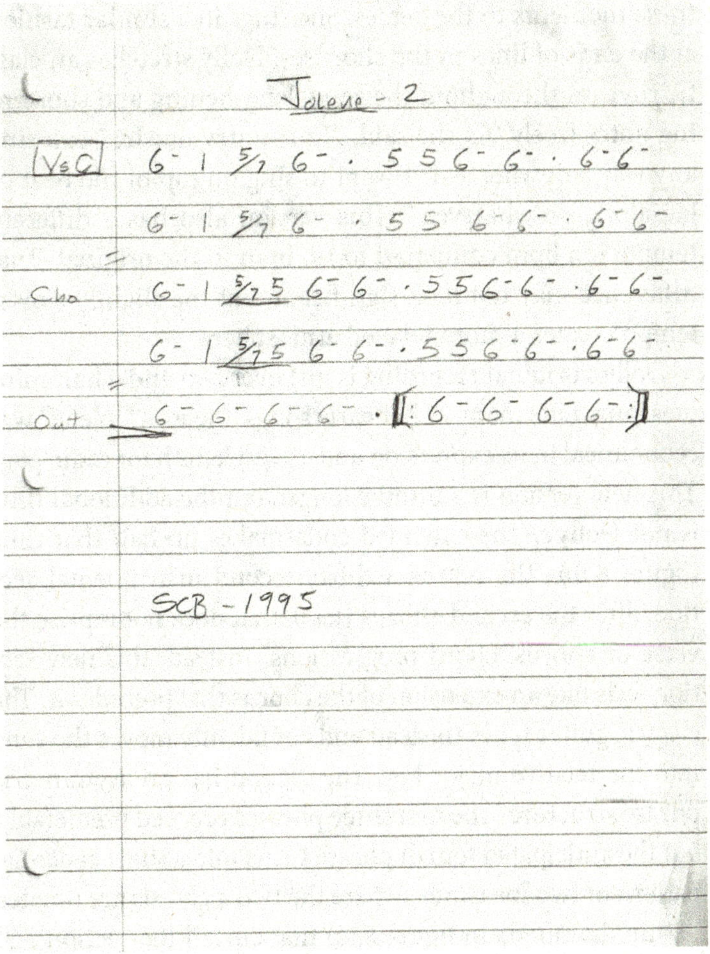

FIGURE 8.1b Dolly Parton, "Jolene," *Something Special*, 1995, studio chart by and courtesy of Steve Buckingham.

1st scale degree, going a whole step below the tonic, as she does on the line "eyes of emerald green."

At that same line, Dolly also elongates the rhythm compared to her original. At the ends of lines, she abandons an allegiance to the pulse of the beats. Dolly does not limit these moments to the verses. She sings in a similar fashion at the ends of lines in the choruses. Dolly stretches an elastic rhythm throughout the song, lengthening and shortening notes freely. As she said, "In country music, I can sing any way, anywhere—if I want to sing on top of the beat or lag along or whatever."[2] This version also has a different tempo: 104 bpm compared to 110 bpm in the original. That difference may not look significant, but the slightly slower tempo creates a more relaxed atmosphere.

Dolly's original recording is just over two and a half minutes long. Like many of her early songs, the 1974 "Jolene" was economical in its expression and a great length for radio play. This new version is a minute longer, but the additional time is not Dolly's. The extended coda makes up half that time (figure 8.1b). The rest is a thirty-second instrumental section, after the second chorus (1:48), that does not reprise the verse or chorus' chord progressions. Instead, this new section feels like an extension of the chorus that precedes it. The electric guitar takes the lead and confidently moves the song into the relative major key. The section has an asymmetric phrase structure. The first three phrases proceed predictably, but the anticipated fourth phrase turns into a short cadential pattern of two measures (where the two 4 chords are notated within diamonds in figure 8.1a) that curtail the section and give way to the familiar guitar riff that kicks off verse 3 (2:01).

This abrupt shift is a nice touch: with this added section, the song had opened up for moment into new territory with new melodic lines and a new key (maybe things will work out for our narrator?), only to quickly and unexpectedly get pulled back into the minor key world of "Jolene." The added instrumental sections combined with Dolly's free approach to rhythm that works tandem with her melodic embellishments give this version a more improvised feeling than her original recording.

DUMPLIN'

Although Dolly does not appear in the 2018 film *Dumplin'*, she and her music are a constant presence since she is a role model for the lead character. Dolly recorded a new version of "Jolene" for the soundtrack recording, though it is not included in the film. This rendition is unlike any of her previous recordings or performances of the song. The song is accompanied by a doubled string quartet (4 violins, 2 violas, 2 cellos), slowed down from 110 bpm to 87 bpm, and strongly tilts toward the Dorian mode instead of Aeolian. (View and listen to examples 8.4a and 8.4b ▶.)

Dolly explained that the song's producer, Linda Perry, modeled this arrangement on "Eleanor Rigby."[3] (Listen to example 8.5 ▶.) Both songs embody alienation and loss. The Beatles portray existential and societal disconnection broadly, while Dolly reflects on an individual's heartbreak. But they both mine the same vein of loneliness. The intimacy of the string accompaniment and the Dorian modal inflection borrowed from "Eleanor Rigby,"[4] combined with the slower tempo, create a haunting and pensive atmosphere in this version of "Jolene."

Only one element of the original accompaniment is retained: a reimagined version of the opening riff (example 8.1). The cellos hold a drone on the tonic note while the violas and violins play smooth but syncopated lines reminiscent of the lick on the guitar. Two violins

EXAMPLE 8.1 Dolly Parton, "Jolene," *Dumplin'* soundtrack (2018), opening guitar riff on strings.

also play a tremolo that enliven the energy of that motive. This orchestration of the guitar riff (sometimes minus the tremolo) appears throughout the song, punctuating ends of lines and sections as in the original.

The arrangement is gently polyphonic; chords give way to suspensions, and countermelodies float above rhythmic interior lines. The opening riff is heard within this texture at the ends of lines, often as an evanescent inner voice, and sometimes abbreviated, as in verse 1 (0:40) (example 8.2). Additionally, the Dorian mode sonority is strong in this section, with the raised 6th scale degrees (A♯). The second verse continues this atmospheric setting.

The second chorus opens with staccato and marcato chords, and the rhythm becomes more insistent (1:35) (example 8.3). This gesture is a direct reference to the string writing in the Beatles' song heard after its intro. And, like the instrumentals in the intro of "Eleanor Rigby," in "Jolene," this pulsing rhythm remains in the cello as the violins and violas shift to counter-melodies and drop in the song's opening riff. A particularly nice touch is the way this

EXAMPLE 8.2 Dolly Parton, "Jolene," *Dumplin'* soundtrack (2018), string parts, verse 1.

riff works with the upper line that connects the phrases by continuing past the cadences (on *man* and *can*).

For her part, Dolly beautifully matches the introspective atmosphere of the orchestration. Her voice is not as light and clear as it was in earlier recordings, although she still has the same vocal control. Some of her musical choices echo those from her re-recording on *Something Special*: she improvises and embellishes her original melody with vocal ornaments; she plays with the rhythm of the lines, especially stretching the ends of lines; and she slides between notes to heighten the emotional effect. But in this version, she pushes each of these elements even more. Her melodies

EXAMPLE 8.3 Dolly Parton, "Jolene," *Dumplin'* soundtrack (2018), string parts, chorus 2.

feel improvised as she lingers on and draws out phrases, particularly on the name Jolene at the ends of lines. Her melodic and rhythmic variants are particularly evident in the third chorus (2:34). Dolly's vocal quality and musical choices, combined with the orchestration, create a world-weary, melancholic yearning rather than the immediate, nervous urgency of her 1974 recording.

Dolly said when she recorded the song "it was really a magical moment. To hear it slowed down that way with the orchestra it really took it into that Elizabethan sound."[5] In another interview she said this version of was "haunting . . ., like some ol' Elizabethan-age music. . . . I thought it turned out really nice."[6] Dolly's description in two interviews of her all-strings version of "Jolene" as *Elizabethan* is striking. The "Elizabethan myth" has been attached to Appalachia for over a century, and, in 1977, Chet Flippo of *Rolling Stone* used the term to describe Dolly's Appalachian musical sound and heritage.[7] Critics picked up the term and have used it ever since. However, Dolly never used that term then or in the intervening years. So, it is unusual that she would describe her strings-only version of "Jolene" as *Elizabethan*.

Perhaps Dolly felt she needed a word for this new sound and used the term that she knew others had before, as she revealed in a 1976 interview. When asked then whether her music has an Appalachian influence, she replied, "I don't really know what causes that, because . . . people that know music technically . . . say that my music is so reminiscent to the old songs, like the old Elixabethan [*sic*] age, but I don't know why or where that comes from, but I know we used to sing old mountain songs."[8] The term *Elizabethan* certainly conjures up an old-world sound, which brings us full circle from those earlier critics who fancifully linked the term to her original recording of "Jolene." Their references—Elizabethan and "Greensleeves"—are English, and the

"Eleanor Rigby"–inspired, Dorian-mode string arrangement extends that English connection enough that Dolly also speaks about this new rendition of "Jolene" using this same "old-world" term, *Elizabethan*.

Dolly has said for decades that her music is influenced by English, Scottish, Irish, and Welsh music. This version of "Jolene" extends and refocuses her notions of this influence, as if it were viewed through a kaleidoscope with all her old-world songs. In this way, her strings-only version of "Jolene" is not an outlier. Her comments about the old-world resonances of its arrangement suggest that she believes its style is adjacent to her other music: it draws on the influences that she claims shape much of her music while moving into new territory. This may be why her recording does not seem pretentious, as if she were putting on a completely alien style. Instead, she approaches the recording in terms of the roots she embraces for her musical identity.

Dolly also described this "Jolene" as "chamber music."[9] In that context, consider her comments at the time of the recording's release: "Jolene's been on the prowl a long time. But she just got a makeover and I couldn't be more excited to share the new string version with y'all!"[10] What is a makeover? It is more than simply a different version. A makeover also suggests transformation, refinement, and a rise in status: like changing your appearance with new hair and makeup to create a more glamorous, even high-class, image. For this version of "Jolene," the classical music–sounding string arrangement is the fashionable new hair and makeup. As Dolly might say, in this version, she has gone uptown. Its genre-crossing classical music atmosphere takes it out of the sound world of a pop song, changing the mood and making it seem more serious. It also creates a timeless quality.

"Jolene" has been with Dolly for fifty years. She has performed it countless times, usually as we expect: with the driving guitar lick and the upbeat, sing-along chorus of the original. But speaking about this all-strings version, Dolly said it was "refreshing actually to get to do it differently than I always have."[11]

HEARTSTRINGS

Dolly's songwriting encompasses dozens of characters, among them a little girl who needed a coat, an abandoned young pregnant woman in Dover, people who work 9 to 5, a neglected little girl and her puppy, and someone who will always love us. And then there is Jolene. Her legendary character topped the list of stories that Dolly included in her eight-part series on Netflix, *Heartstrings*, in 2019.

In the episode about "Jolene," Dolly explored the relationship between the narrator and Jolene that the song can only suggest. It weaves in several of the issues that I have raised in my study of the song: the possibility of a homoerotic reading of the dynamic between the two women; the absence of the man in their encounter; and the question of what Jolene will decide. Before I discuss how the episode deals with these points, a brief plot outline is in order (with spoilers).

As the story opens, we meet Babe (played by Dolly) who owns a local honky tonk. Jolene—red-headed, bare shoulders and midriff, short shorts, cowboy boots—works there tending bar, waitressing, and singing in the nightly show.

She was recently fired from her day job as a bank teller for flirting with customers. Babe is Jolene's mentor. She believes Jolene has the talent to be a successful country singer and encourages her to go to Nashville. Jolene keeps putting it off, seemingly content in the small town, but actually scared to put herself to the test. Into this scenario walks Emily, an attractive late-thirty-something wife and mother. Her attempt at perking up her lackluster marriage with a date night with her husband has failed. When he begs off, she strikes up a conversation with Jolene and is instantly taken with her, openly admiring Jolene's beauty and talent. When Emily is assaulted that night by a creepy, vulgar man outside the women's restroom, Jolene comes to her rescue. The two instantly become friends.

As their friendship develops, Emily reveals that her marriage has gone stale; she no longer feels sexually desirable to her husband. Jolene helps with fashion advice and some pointers about sexual role-playing, but Emily's efforts fall flat with her husband. Soon after that, Jolene tells Emily she is having an affair with a married man (the husband of one of Emily's friends, it turns out). She explains she is a free spirit who wants no emotional entanglements. Soon Emily fears Jolene will go after her husband, and she starts avoiding Jolene. Eventually Emily confronts Jolene about her suspicions, which are unfounded. But their relationship is broken.

Babe senses the troubles Jolene has and insists that Jolene go to Nashville by firing her from the bar. Babe also makes sure that Emily learns Jolene is leaving. She runs to the bus station to say goodbye, but just misses Jolene by a few moments. The women exchange text messages wishing each other well. The film ends two years later with Jolene a successful singer in Nashville. Emily and her husband have come to see her show, apparently having saved their marriage. The women are reunited (the husband goes to get a drink), and they confirm their strong friendship. All ends happily.

The surface narrative of the episode remains true to expectations: Jolene is a woman who sleeps with married men, and the narrator feels threatened by her. But this television version more deeply explores the friendship between the two women, which tilts close to the vibe suggested by those who read lesbian eroticism in "Jolene." Emily openly admires Jolene; she looks at her adoringly and shyly asks about her confidence: "how are you, *you*?" (figure 8.2).

In the scene when Emily reveals doubts about her sexual attractiveness, the two women's body language is intimate. Emily continues her admiration of Jolene, who leans up

FIGURE 8.2 Dolly Parton's *Heartstrings*, "Jolene" episode, Emily looking at Jolene.

against Emily on the couch, brushes a lock of hair from Emily's face, flops across Emily's lap to get more wine, and smacks Emily on the butt as they adjourn to the bedroom to look at Emily's beige wardrobe in preparation for a Jolene-led makeover and advice about sexual role-playing. One critic sensed what I had: "my attention zoned in on the connection between charismatic Jolene . . . and the simmering wife . . ., and I fully expected these women to passionately kiss. In fact, I was pretty disappointed when they didn't."[12] Neither veered from her lane.

The actress who played Emily commented about her character's strong attachment to Jolene, "who threatens everything, and yet everyone seems to be in love with. . . . She's this magnetic, amazing person, so I loved playing that tension between loving her and then being threatened by her as well."[13] Emily's admiration of Jolene is at center of their eventual confrontation scene, and the lyrics of the song fuel their encounter. Emily asks Jolene if she is sleeping with her husband. When Jolene truthfully denies it, Emily said she has a hard time believing her because "you have affairs with married men just because you can." Jolene replies, "I would never do that to you." (View example 8.6 ▶.)

EMILY: "Well then why is he saying your name in his sleep? (*Jolene shakes her head.*) Why is he telling me he's working, and I know he's at your bar?"

JOLENE: "I don't know. Honestly, what did he say when you asked him?"

EMILY: (*Rolls her eyes and shakes her head.*)

Jolene (*angrily*): "Wait!! You didn't even ask him? Instead of confronting your husband you just shut me out? Why? I wanna know why!"

Emily (*whimpering*): "Because . . . look at you! You're like this perfect flower. (*Leaning in to Jolene; talking faster.*) And you smell perfect. And your voice is like. . . ."

Jolene (*interrupting her*): "What are you even saying?"

Emily: "I'm saying that I can't compete with you Jolene! I'm saying my marriage, my happiness, my everything depends on you! And so I'm asking you, woman to woman, stay away. Please."

This encounter flips the script of the song: that Jolene is stealing another woman's man and that she has all the power. Here we have a different story. Jolene has formed a close friendship with Emily, whose loving admiration of Jolene causes her to project her feelings onto her husband. She then assumes he is sleeping with Jolene (because who wouldn't!?). In this scenario, Jolene is the wronged member of the triangle. She was the one faithful to the friendship, not Emily whose own insecurities caused her to doubt Jolene. At the end of this scene, both women are heartbroken at the ending of their friendship, but it is Jolene who has been betrayed. Jolene began their conversation saying, "I would never do that to you"—betray a friend—and her anger and pain at the end of the scene is because Emily *did* do that to her.

Another element in this scene is the revelation that Emily has not spoken to her husband. It is a sign of their weak marriage that she does not talk to him about her suspicions. But it is also a way that Emily can blame someone outside of the marriage for their problems. Jolene knows this. The situation echoes the remark by Chapel Hart singer Trea about their answer song, "You Can Have Him Jolene": "the reality is that 'it's not just me and you honey, it's me, you *and* him. We *all* gotta talk about it.' He's part of it too."[14]

Even though women are the center of the narrative, the show also critiques men's behaviors. Emily's husband is initially unwilling to attend to his marriage, and he rebuffs all her attempts to work on their relationship, although he fantasizes briefly about Jolene. Then there is Hugh, the married man Jolene was sleeping with. When Emily chided Jolene about this, Jolene was not having it: "He's married. I'm not. I'm not the one doing the cheating." When Hugh's wife learns about the affair, she attends a concert of Jolene's and shouts "whore!" as Jolene prepares to sing. Stunned but stalwart, Jolene pivots to a different song, "Just Because I'm a Woman," written by Dolly.[15] The song challenges the sexual double standard: "my mistakes are no worse than yours, just because I'm a woman." At this moment in the story, Jolene fights back through a song that echoes the sentiments of Kitty Wells's "It Wasn't God Who Made Honky Tonk Angels": all the blame should not be put on women. If cheating husbands were not enough, the episode starts with a man accosting Emily in the bar.

At the episode's end, Emily and her husband have recommitted to their marriage, though we do not see any of the work that entailed. Instead, the focus remains on the women's friendship, which is the primary relationship in the story. Their reconciliation is demonstrated through

Jolene's performance of another song by Dolly, "Something Special," sung directly to Emily.[16] (Listen to example 8.7 ▶.)

> When I'm around you
> The love that surrounds you
> Brings comfort and warmth to my heart
> You are a true friend
> . . .
> Like the song that they sing
> You're the wind 'neath my wings
> There are so many things that you've been
> An angel in my life
> You're rainbows and sunlight
> I hope we'll always be friends
> 'Cause you're special (spoken)

The lyrics are Jolene's reciprocal answer to Emily's lines, "your beauty is beyond compare. . . ."

With this version of the song's story, Dolly adds another possibility to how we might understand Jolene. Previously, we saw various ways of imagining Jolene in the answer songs. She might be a villain, even one who "can have him." But she might also be an unwitting participant in the adulterous relationship. She might even protect the narrator by warning her about her unfaithful partner. In all the answer songs, Jolene was, at least at some point, involved with the narrator's man. In this "answer song to herself,"[17] Dolly gives us a Jolene who is more faithful to the narrator than any of the other Jolenes we have encountered. Her loyalty is to her friend, and that is an unexpected, but welcome answer to the question, "what does Jolene decide?"[18]

CHAPTER 9

RETURNING TO JOLENE

THE TRADITIONAL ORIGIN STORY of "Jolene" is that Dolly had a run-in with a red-headed bank teller who was flirting with her husband. Dolly always uses this humorous, presumably autobiographical account to introduce the song. But she coyly cautioned her audience not to put too much stock in this story when she sang "Jolene" at the celebration for her fiftieth anniversary as a member of the Grand Ole Opry. She said the song was "based on a thread of truth, but it was so frayed by the time I got finished with it, it didn't even matter."[1]

I want to return to the other origin story about the little red-headed, green-eyed girl named "Jolene," whom Dolly met after a show and whose name inspired the song. As Dolly sang the name over and over, she thought, "What am I going to write about 'Jolene'? I have to have a real commercial story

Dolly Parton's Jolene. Lydia R. Hamessley, Oxford University Press. © Oxford University Press 2025.
DOI: 10.1093/9780197760345.003.0010

so it'd get played on the radio." Shima Oliaee summed up Dolly's point: "The bank teller jealousy thing, that was just the commercial wrapping." But Dolly's real inspiration for the song, "the bigger deal," was little Jolene.[2]

Dolly's encounter with little Jolene brings to mind something Dolly once said about her dear friend Judy Ogle. The two girls met in the third grade. They instantly became best friends and have been inseparable most of their lives. Judy is Dolly's personal assistant, and they "have been as close as any two sisters could ever hope to be."[3] Dolly says, "I love her as much as I love anybody in the whole world."[4]

In her autobiography Dolly writes about meeting Judy. "I was drawn to her because of her big green cat-curious eyes. I was also fascinated by her hair, the color of a new copper penny."[5] This sounds a lot like Jolene. Did Dolly see her friend Judy in the little girl seeking an autograph, who was also about the same age as Judy when she met Dolly? And might Dolly have written the first verse ("your beauty is beyond compare with flaming locks of auburn hair . . . and eyes of emerald green") with Judy in mind as well as little Jolene and bank teller Jolene?

There is a further aspect of the story about the little girl seeking an autograph that flies under the radar: she was wearing a Girl Scout uniform.[6] Girls her age were Junior Scouts, and, at that time, she would have been wearing the green dress with badge sash, yellow bow tie, green beret, and green socks. This outfit would have set off little Jolene's red hair and green eyes beautifully (figure 9.1).

Dolly's recollection of how she felt seeing that uniform on little Jolene is noteworthy: "You know, she's probably a poor girl like me and if I'd been a Girl Scout that would

FIGURE 9.1 Girl Scout uniforms, circa 1963–1973.

have been the greatest thing in the world, to have a complete outfit to dress up in. Her hair was auburn like in the song, and she was just so pretty."[7] Dolly felt a connection to little Jolene, whom she imagined was poor as Dolly had been. But this little girl also had a wonderful uniform to wear, a "complete outfit," not a hodgepodge of hand-me-downs and patched clothing that Dolly had worn, as she describes in "Coat of Many Colors."

My own recollections of wearing this same uniform in the mid- and late 1960s help me understand Dolly's feelings. I had yearned to be a Girl Scout when I saw other girls wearing that uniform. Joining a troop and wearing such a distinctive outfit complete with symbolic insignia and proudly earned merit badges was a great feeling. I felt important and somehow significant. Keeping this seemingly small detail of the Girl Scout uniform in mind adds to the richness of Dolly's Jolene story and augments the emotions imbued in the song. Dolly's first feelings associated with Jolene included a yearning to have what that little green-eyed, red-headed girl had: not a man, but a beautiful outfit that made the wearer special and mitigated her presumed poverty.

Dolly's sparkling image is one way she transcended the poverty of her youth: "The reason I like my hair and pretty clothes is it's something I never had as a kid. . . . As children, we had to wear britches with the hind end out of them and patches all over. The faded denim and stringy hair and scrubbed faces. It was fine, but we had no choice. So then, I automatically thought when I get grown up, I'm going to have pretty clothes and pretty jewelry and pretty make-up and pretty hair-dos. I wanted to know what it feels like."[8] Dolly's glamorous look demonstrates upward mobility (as she often says, "It takes a lot of money to look this cheap"). Thus, in the song, Jolene's beauty might also be a sign of her class superiority that impoverishes the singer in comparison. In this context, we can understand "Jolene" as another of Dolly's songs that is shaped by her childhood poverty, which she yearned to escape.

"No human being cannot be affected by 'Jolene.'"[9] Tokyo Sexwale's ardent statement captures the influence and ubiquity of the song. In talking with people while writing about Dolly, I have found that the average listener will name "Jolene," "I Will Always Love You," or "9 to 5" when asked for a Dolly song. "Jolene" usually tops the list.

Dolly continues to explore and reimagine "Jolene," more than these other songs, through new arrangements, collaborations, and dramatic interpretations. As our rummage through my Jolene collection reveals, "Jolene" has traveled the furthest beyond Dolly's world. It shows up in images, movies, memes, short stories, and television shows. In covers and answer songs, artists from across different gender, sexual, racial, ethnic, and national identities bring an array of readings to "Jolene," whose central character remains an enigma.

As one critic pointed out a couple of years after the song's release, it is "puzzling . . . that in the finished product Jolene emerged as a threat ("*please don't take my man*"), whereas in Dolly's experience the little girl existed as a figure of innocence. Even reminding Dolly of herself at [that] age."[10] Innocence. Not the first word that comes to mind with "Jolene." However, Dolly once said, "It's really an innocent song all around, but sounds like a dreadful one."[11] So perhaps little Jolene and best friends little Judy and little Dolly are just as much at the emotional center of the song as the mythical red-headed bank teller.

NOTES

ACKNOWLEDGMENTS

1. Abbie Kozolchyk, "Dolly Parton's 'Jolene' Is 50: Why Her Most Covered Song Has Enduring Global Appeal," *Los Angeles Times*, February 29, 2024, https://www.latimes.com/entertainment-arts/music/story/2024-02-29/dolly-partons-jolene-is-50-why-her-most-covered-song-has-enduring-global-appeal.

INTRODUCTION

1. Beyoncé's recording was released just as this book was going into production.
2. Shannon Larson, "'Vaccine, vaccine, vaccine, vacciiiine': Northeastern Professor Performs Rendition of Dolly Parton's Hit," *Boston Globe*, November 28, 2020, https://www.bostonglobe.com/2020/11/18/metro/vaccine-vaccine-vaccine-vacciiiine-northeastern-professor-performs-rendition-dolly-partons-hit/.
3. Andrew Kurjata and Jordan Tucker, "Could a British Columbia Nurse Be Dolly Parton's Jolene?," *CBC News*, August 24, 2016, http://www.cbc.ca/news/canada/british-columbia/dolly-parton-s-jolene-may-be-a-british-columbia-nurse-1.3734082.
4. https://www.paretewalls.com/walls/p/bsvi-08-jolene.
5. Annie Zaleski, "Dolly Parton's 'Jolene': Why the Other-Woman Heart-to-Heart Is Her Most Popular, Iconic Song," *The Boot*, October 15, 2021, https://theboot.com/dolly-parton-jolene-legacy/.
6. Carena Liptak, "35 Greatest Country Cheating Songs, Ranked," *Taste of Country*, August 9, 2023, https://tasteofcountry.com/cheating-songs/.

7. Jad Abumrad and Shima Oliaee, "The Only One for Me, Jolene," *Dolly Parton's America*, episode 6, November 19, 2019, https://www.wnycstudios.org/podcasts/dolly-partons-america/episodes/only-one-me-jolene.
8. Zaleski, "Dolly Parton's 'Jolene.'"

CHAPTER 1

1. Dolly Parton, *The Bobby Bones Show*, October 9, 2017, https://www.youtube.com/watch?v=z48gLpOn_SA.
2. Alanna Nash, "Dolly Parton: Sitting Pretty," *Journal of Country Music* 23, no. 3 (2004): 12.
3. "Dolly Parton Replies to Fans on the Internet | Actually Me | GQ," *GQ: Actually Me*, November 11, 2020, https://www.youtube.com/watch?v=XjumLoAfOjo.
4. Mayer Nissim, "'Jolene' by Dolly Parton: The Making of the Pleading Country Classic," *Gold Radio*, January 31, 2022, https://www.goldradiouk.com/news/music/jolene-dolly-parton-song-facts-real-person/.
5. Robert K. Oermann, "Dolly Parton: Here She Comes Again," *Country Sounds*, May 1987, 6.
6. All references in the text to chart positions are for the *Billboard* Country Chart unless otherwise noted.
7. *Billboard*, "Top Album Picks," 86, no. 7 (February 16, 1974): 50.
8. Bob Adels, "The Year's Best Records: One Man's Opinion," *Country Music Beat* 1, no. 1 (1974): 52.
9. "Dolly Parton—*Coat of Many Colors/My Tennessee Mountain Home/Jolene*," *No Depression*, May 1, 2007, https://www.nodepression.com/album-reviews/dolly-parton-coat-of-many-colors-my-tennessee-mountain-home-jolene/.
10. Dave Heaton, "Growing Up Hurts: Dolly Parton's Albums of 'Independence," *Pop Matters*, May 16, 2007, https://www.popmatters.com/growing-up-hurts-dolly-partons-2496212339.html.
11. Alanna Nash, *Dolly: The Biography*, updated edition (New York: Cooper Square Press, 2002), 137.
12. Nash, *Dolly: The Biography*, 137.
13. "Dolly Parton Branches Off in New Direction," *Camden News*, November 11, 1976, 9.
14. The B side of the "Jolene" single (released October 15, 1973) was "Love, You're So Beautiful Tonight," written by Porter Wagoner. That 45 rpm had both groups: the heartbreak on Side A, the happiness on Side B.
15. Dolly re-recorded "Barbara on Your Mind" in a different arrangement for her 1982 album *Heartbreak Express*.

CHAPTER 2

1. Dolly Parton quoted in Tom Vitale, "Dolly Parton's 'Jolene' Still Haunts Singers," *All Things Considered*, NPR (October 9, 2008), http://www.npr.org/2008/10/09/95520570/dolly-partons-jolene-still-haunts-singers.
2. Parton quoted in Vitale, "Dolly Parton's 'Jolene.'"
3. Parton quoted in Abumrad and Oliaee, *Dolly Parton's America*, episode 6.
4. Parton quoted in Abumrad and Oliaee, *Dolly Parton's America*, episode 6.
5. *Barbara Walters Special*, aired December 6, 1977, on ABC. Thanks to Ryan Hayes for reminding me of this connection.
6. Eve Kosofsky Sedgwick, *Between Men: English Literature and Male Homosocial Desire* (New York: Columbia University Press, 1985), 21.
7. Nash, *Dolly: The Biography*, 136.
8. Apparently, she was using "china" to mean a shade of off-white or beige frequently known as "china doll," a name that paint company Sherwin-Williams has now retired.
9. Dolly made another significant change in the lyrics of verse 2 (figure 2.1b). She originally wrote:

   It's not that I don't understand
   He is a very special man
   But I'm the one that wears his ring Jolene.

   She then scrapped her first draft for the more euphonious lyrics of the song as we know it:

   I can easily understand
   How you could easily take my man
   But you don't know what he means to me Jolene.

   Although her revision is a stronger lyric, what was lost in this change is the revelation that the singer is married (or engaged) to her man. Nowhere else in the song is the specific nature of their relationship defined, which contributes to the song's ambiguity.
10. Lydia R. Hamessley, *Unlikely Angel: The Songs of Dolly Parton* (Urbana: University of Illinois Press, 2020), 56, 66–70.
11. Kate Heidemann, "Remarkable Women and Ordinary Gals: Performance of Identity in Songs by Loretta Lynn and Dolly Parton," in *Country Boys and Redneck Women: New Essays in Gender and Country Music*, ed. Diane Pecknold and Kristine M. McCusker (Jackson: University Press of Mississippi, 2016), 167 and 171.
12. Nadine Hubbs, "'Jolene,' Genre, and the Everyday Homoerotics of Country Music: Dolly Parton's Loving Address of the Other Woman," *Women & Music: A Journal of Gender and Culture* 19 (2015): 74.
13. Steve Eng, *A Satisfied Mind: The Country Music Life of Porter Wagoner* (Nashville: Rutledge Hill Press, 1992), 320.

14. Zaleski, "Dolly Parton's 'Jolene.'"
15. Jim Beviglia, "Lyric of the Week: Dolly Parton, 'Jolene,'" July 28, 2014, https://americansongwriter.com/2014/07/lyric-week-dolly-parton-jolene/.
16. Hamessley, *Unlikely Angel*, 122–23.
17. Laura Cunningham, "Dolly Parton: The Supersexy Superstar of Country Pop," *Cosmopolitan* 186 (January 1979): 134. Emphasis and ellipses following "Listen" in original.
18. Cunningham, "Dolly Parton," 134.
19. Beviglia, "Lyric of the Week."
20. Hubbs, "'Jolene,' Genre, and the Everyday Homoerotics of Country Music," 72, 75, 72.
21. Abumrad and Oliaee, *Dolly Parton's America*, episode 6.
22. Sappho, "Fragment 31," in *Sappho: A New Translation*, trans. Mary Barnard (Oakland: University of California Press, 2019).
23. Parton quoted in Abumrad and Oliaee, *Dolly Parton's America*, episode 6.
24. Hamessley, *Unlikely Angel*, 123–24 and 193–97.
25. "I Kissed a Girl," *Glee*, season 3, episode 7, aired November 29, 2011, on Fox.
26. Spoiler: these issues are further complicated several seasons later in the show when Coach Beiste comes out as transgender.
27. Sydney Miller, "Ten Supremely Sapphic Country Songs," *Country Queer*, October 9, 2020, https://countryqueer.com/stories/list/the-most-sapphic-songs-from-your-favorite-lesbian-artists/.
28. The film is based on the novel by Julie Murphy, *Dumplin'* (New York: Balzer + Bray, 2015).
29. *Dolly*, season 1, episode 1, aired January 10, 1988 on ABC.
30. Porter Wagoner quoted in Porter Wagoner and Glenn Hunter, "Hello Dolly," *Journal of Country Music* 10, no. 1 (1985): 16.
31. Parton quoted in Vitale, "Dolly Parton's 'Jolene.'"
32. Zaleski, "Dolly Parton's 'Jolene.'"

CHAPTER 3

1. Jack Hurst, "You've Come a Long Way, Dolly," *Hi Fidelity Magazine* (December 1977): 123.
2. Jean Vallely, "On the Rock Road with Dolly Parton," *Time* 109, no. 16 (April 18, 1977): 72.
3. Nash, *Dolly: The Biography*, 136.
4. Tom Carson, "Dolly Parton Breaks a Heart [release of *Heartbreaker*]," *Rolling Stone*, October 19, 1978, 92–93, https://www.rollingstone.com/music/music-country/heartbreaker-93765/.

5. Hurst, "You've Come a Long Way, Dolly," 124.
6. Dolly Parton quoted in Hurst, "You've Come a Long Way, Dolly," 123.
7. "Dolly Parton Reveals: The Real Story Behind the Name 'Jolene,'" https://www.youtube.com/watch?v=4olTHrogUoE.
8. Eng, *A Satisfied Mind*, 320.
9. Eng, *A Satisfied Mind*, 320.
10. Nash, *Dolly: The Biography*, 136.
11. I write extensively about the use of the term *Elizabethan* to describe much of Dolly's music in *Unlikely Angel*, 89–96.
12. Dolly Parton, personal communication, 2018. See Hamessley, *Unlikely Angel*, 70–71.
13. Hubbs, "'Jolene,' Genre, and the Everyday Homoerotics of Country Music," 74; Heidemann, "Remarkable Women," 179 and 187.
14. See Hamessley, *Unlikely Angel*, for an in-depth discussion of Dolly's use of modes, especially 70–74 and 235–238.
15. Dolly Parton quoted in Mat Snow, "American Idol," *Mojo Music Magazine* 175 (June 2008): 64.
16. Hildegard von Blingin' is a send-up of the medieval abbess and composer Hildegard von Bingen (1098–1179) who wrote liturgical songs and chants collected in *Symphonia armoniae celestium revelationum*.
17. Vitale, "Dolly Parton's 'Jolene.'"
18. Dolly Parton quoted in Carolyn Allen, "The Dolly Parton Interview: Candy Kicker Meets Cinderella," *Picking Up the Tempo: A Country Western Journal* 13 (December/January 1976): 3, https://digi.countrymusichalloffame.org/digital/collection/Printed/id/3418/rec/23.
19. Parton quoted in Abumrad and Oliaee, *Dolly Parton's America*, episode 6.
20. Parton quoted in Vitale, "Dolly Parton's 'Jolene.'"
21. Although I transcribe the riff in 4/4, Nashville studio musicians consider a measure the equivalent of two bass notes. Following that practice, the song would be notated in cut time or what these musicians call "fast 4" (see an example later in figure 8.1), and the guitar riff would be two measures long. But since the riff occurs over four beats, it is clearer to see the rhythmic relationships I discuss with the beats notated with quarter notes without the interruption of a bar line. In practice, the lick is played at a tempo of 110 bpm that implies cut time, that is, two beats per measure.
22. I recorded the riff slowly in A minor instead of C♯ minor so that the pitches I refer to in my analysis match the written pitch of the transcription and recording.
23. Kate Heidemann, *Hearing Women's Voices in Popular Song: Analyzing Sound and Identity in Country and Soul* (PhD diss., Columbia University, 2014), 165. Heidemann does not untangle the three polyphonic strands or the

cross-rhythm and polyrhythm in her analysis, but she hears the same effects, which she describes as a "sense of the music passing by in an uneven cycle."

24. Parton quoted in Vitale, "Dolly Parton's 'Jolene.'"
25. Lauren Matthews, "People Can't Stop Sharing This Adorable Video of a Toddler Singing 'Jolene," *Country Living*, January 24, 2017, https://www.countryliving.com/life/kids-pets/a41455/baby-sings-jolene-video/.
26. Hamessley, *Unlikely Angel*, 121.
27. Parton quoted in Vitale, "Dolly Parton's 'Jolene.'"
28. Alternatively, the verse could be heard as four lines long, with the a and a′ lines making up the first and third phrases that are analogous to the first and third phrases of the chorus (when the name "Jolene" is sung), and with the b lines analogous to the chorus's second and fourth phrases. However, the first two lines of the verse (a and a′) run directly into the third line (b) with no sense of pause or arrival to strongly mark the first two lines as a separate phrase.
29. In her original, hand-written lyrics (figure 2.1), Dolly indicates a chorus at the top of the second sheet, between verses 1 and 2, and she does not specify a chorus between verses 2 and 3. She also indicates that the chorus should be sung twice at the end of the song. But it is clear these lyrics were dashed off quickly. The final form of the song was likely developed in the studio.
30. Heidemann, "Remarkable Women," 178.
31. Parton quoted in Hurst, "You've Come a Long Way, Dolly," 124.
32. Heidemann, "Remarkable Women," 178.
33. Noel Coppage, "Dolly," *Stereo Review* 43, no. 3 (September 1979): 84.

CHAPTER 4

1. Bill Anderson quoted in Jerry Bailey, "Country Music Group Defended," *The Tennessean*, November 15, 1974, 22.
2. Johnny Paycheck quoted in Jerry Bailey, "Group Misunderstands CMA: Member," *The Tennessean*, November 14, 1974, 36.
3. Billy Walker quoted in Bailey, "Country Music Group Defended."
4. Billy Walker quoted in "Nashville Singers' Gripe: It's Influx of 'These People,'" *The* (Utica, NY) *Observer-Dispatch*, November 29, 1974, 55.
5. Barbara Mandrell quoted in "Strict Ethics Code Bared by ACE at Its Nashville Seminar," *Billboard* 87, no. 13 (March 29, 1975): 38.
6. Anderson quoted in Bailey, "Country Music Group Defended."
7. J. R. Young, "Olivia Newton-John, Country Singer. What?" *Country* Music 3, no. 3 (December 1974): 62.

8. Annie Zaleski, "Olivia Newton-John's Catalog of Emotion," *Oxford American* 119 (Winter 2022), https://oxfordamerican.org/magazine/issue-119-winter-2022/olivia-newtonjohn-s-catalog-of-emotion.
9. Robert Windeler, "Olivia Newton-John Is the Pop and Country Star Without a Country," *People*, February 24, 1975, 39.
10. Olivia Newton-John quoted in Tim Ewbank, *Olivia: The Biography of Olivia Newton-John* (London: Piatkus, 2008), 121.
11. Olivia Newton-John, remarks during her *Physical* Tour at Weber State University, Ogden, Utah, October 12, 1982.
12. Ewbank, *Olivia*, 118.
13. Olivia Newton-John, *Don't Stop Believin'* (New York: Gallery Books, 2018), 70.
14. Parton quoted in Nash, *Dolly: The Biography*, 149. Dolly's sister Stella Parton was angered by what she viewed as a hypocritical position of those in ACE, several of whom had also come into country music from pop or rock backgrounds. In 1975, she wrote "Ode to Olivia," which wove titles from Newton-John's songs into the lyrics, and included the declaration, "we ain't got the right to say you're not country." (Listen to example 4.8 ▶.)
15. Dolly Parton quoted in "Olivia Newton John Wins Pop/Rock Female Artist—AMA 1977," https://www.youtube.com/watch?v=9-gul7O1ifk.
16. John Rockwell, "'I Am Dolly Parton From the Mountains . . . I Am Country,'" *New York Times*, November 19, 1976, 70.
17. Dolly Parton, *Dolly: My Life and Other Unfinished Business* (New York: HarperCollins, 1994), 188.
18. Parton, *Dolly: My Life and Other Unfinished Business*, 189.
19. Dolly Parton quoted in Lawrence Grobel, "Dolly Parton: A Candid Conversation with the Curvaceous Queen of Country Music," *Playboy*, October 1978, 106. Also available in Randy L. Schmidt, ed., *Dolly on Dolly: Interviews and Encounters with Dolly Parton* (Chicago: Chicago Review Press, 2017), 114.
20. Melissa Jun Rowley, "What We Can Learn from Dolly Parton's Business Savvy and Her $1 Million Donation to the Moderna Vaccine to Fight Covid-19," *Forbes*, November 18, 2020, https://www.forbes.com/sites/melissarowley/2020/11/18/what-we-can-learn-from-dolly-partons-business-savvy--her-1-million-donation-to-the-moderna-vaccine-to-fight-covid-19/.
21. Dolly Parton quoted in Stephen Miller, *Smart Blonde: The Life of Dolly Parton* (London: Omnibus Press, 2007), 135.
22. "Olivia & Dolly Parton Team Up for New Duet of 'Jolene,'" February 17, 2023, https://olivianewton-john.com/olivia-dolly-parton-team-up-for-new-duet-of-jolene/.
23. Michael Caprio quoted in "Olivia & Dolly Parton Team Up for New Duet of 'Jolene.'"

CHAPTER 5

1. Clarence Selman quoted in Nash, *Dolly: The Biography*, 138.
2. Beviglia, "Lyric of the Week: Dolly Parton, 'Jolene.'"
3. Abbie Kozolchyk, "Dolly Parton's 'Jolene' Is 50: Why Her Most Covered Song Has Enduring Global Appeal," *Los Angeles Times*, February 29, 2024, https://www.latimes.com/entertainment-arts/music/story/2024-02-29/dolly-partons-jolene-is-50-why-her-most-covered-song-has-enduring-global-appeal.
4. SecondHandSongs, https://secondhandsongs.com/work/27429.
5. Vitale, "Dolly Parton's 'Jolene.'"
6. *The Grass Is Blue* (1999), *Little Sparrow* (2001), and *Halos & Horns* (2002).
7. *The Tonight Show with Jay Leno*, Episode 11.173, October 9, 2003.
8. Jack White quoted in Vitale, "Dolly Parton's 'Jolene.'"
9. Marissa R. Moss, "Jack White: Six Degrees of Nashville," *Rolling Stone*, June 3, 2014, https://www.rollingstone.com/music/music-country/jack-white-six-degrees-of-nashville-85875/.
10. Heran Mamo, "Lil Nas X Brings 'Beautifully Sad' Cover of Dolly Parton's 'Jolene' to BBC Radio 1 Live Lounge, *Billboard*, September 21, 2021, https://www.billboard.com/music/rb-hip-hop/lil-nas-x-dolly-parton-jolene-cover-video-9633392/.
11. Zoe Haylock, "Lil Nas X Goes Back to His Country Roots Covering Dolly Parton's 'Jolene,'" *Vulture*, September 29, 2021, https://www.vulture.com/2021/09/lil-nas-x-covers-jolene-by-dolly-parton-in-the-live-lounge.html.
12. Holyn Thigpen, "Lil Nas X Turns Dolly Parton's 'Jolene' into Haunting and Soulful Tale of Queer Heartbreak, and We're Here For It," *Bust*, September 23, 2021, https://bust.com/lil-nas-x-jolene-cover/.
13. From the bio in their press kit at https://www.congocowboys.com/.
14. Lingala lyrics and translation courtesy of Simon Attwell of The Congo Cowboys.
15. Suzy Exposito, "Chiquis, Becky G Cover Dolly Parton's 'Jolene,'" *Rolling Stone*, June 29, 2020, https://www.rollingstone.com/music/music-latin/chiquis-becky-g-jolene-1020490/.
16. The translation into Spanish is by songwriter Luciano Luna. Thanks to Jessica Burke, Carol A. Hess, and Victoria Betancourt Nieto for help with the translation from Spanish.
17. Dolly Parton on the Latin Recording Academy's *Essal y du música* special, 2021, https://www.youtube.com/watch?v=TeUDOwXs_oA.
18. Tionah Lee, "Becky G and Chiquis Rivera Give a Cumbia Makeover to Dolly Parton's 'Jolene'" *Hola!*, May 29, 2020, https://www.hola.com/us/celebrities/20200529fnvopffwow/becky-g-chiquis-rivera-jolene-single/.

CHAPTER 6

1. *WHT.RBBT.OBJ*, http://www.whtrbbtobj.com/.
2. Kirsty MacColl quoted in Larry Printz, "There Are Twists Galore in Kirsty MacColl's Songs," *The Morning Call*, March 11, 1995, https://www.mcall.com/1995/03/11/there-are-twists-galore-in-kirsty-maccolls-songs/.
3. Jennifer Nettles quoted in "'That Girl' Offers Up a Response to Dolly Parton's 'Jolene'," August 21, 2013, https://www.antimusic.com/news/13/August/21Jennifer_Nettles_That_Girl_Offers_Up_a_Response_to_Dolly_Partons_Jolene.shtml.
4. Nettles quoted in "'That Girl.'"
5. Timothy Yap, "Jennifer Nettles 'That Girl' Review," *JubileeCast*, January 14, 2014, https://jubileecast.com/articles/854/20140114/jennifer-nettles-that-girl-review.htm.
6. Cam quoted in Sterling Whitaker, "Sound Off: Is Cam's 'Diane' a Hit? [Listen]," *Taste of Country*, October 27, 2017, https://tasteofcountry.com/cam-diane/.
7. Megan Bledsoe, "Single Review: Cam's 'Diane,'" October 31, 2017, https://countryexclusive.com/single-review-cams-diane/; and "Song Review—Cam's 'Diane,'" October 30, 2017, https://www.savingcountrymusic.com/song-review-cams-diane/.
8. Cam quoted in Zaleski, "Dolly Parton's 'Jolene.'"
9. Ashley McBryde quoted in Emily Yahr, "A Hit Country Song about a Cheating Man Is Uniting Fans Who've Been There," *Washington Post*, April 4, 2008, https://www.washingtonpost.com/arts-entertainment/2022/04/08/carly-pearce-ashley-mcbryde-never-wanted-be-that-girl/.

CHAPTER 7

1. Danica Hart, interview with the author, August 30, 2023. All quotes from Danica Hart, Devynn Hart, and Trea Swindle are from this interview unless otherwise noted.
2. https://twitter.com/DollyParton/status/1549793699420405760, July 20, 2022.
3. Devynn and Danica Hart quoted in "TOP Songs from Chapel Hart," AGT, https://www.youtube.com/watch?v=XX5L_cHIziQ.
4. Danica Hart and Trea Swindle quoted in Veronica Barriga, "Chapel Hart Breaks Barriers," *Spectrum News 1*, April 4, 2023, https://www.youtube.com/watch?v=UHIY2TsOti8.
5. Trea Swindle quoted in Joey Guerra, "Family Trio Chapel Hart Is Breaking Down Country-Music Barriers," September 28, 2020, https://preview.houstonchronicle.com/music/black-female-country-trio-chapel-hart-breaking-15597606.

6. Devynn takes over singing the lead, and Danica sings harmony in a mid-range with Trea on the lower harmony.
7. Danica Hart and Simon Cowell, *America's Got Talent*, season 17, episode 8, aired July 19, 2022, on NBC.
8. Marcus Dowling, "Chapel Hart on Their Grand Ole Opry Debut, Potential for Acclaim in Country Music," *The Tennessean*, September 19, 2022, https://www.tennessean.com/story/entertainment/2022/09/18/chapel-hart-on-their-grand-ole-opry-debut/69501793007/.
9. Danica Hart quoted in Madeleine O'Connell, "Chapel Hart Bids Farewell to Industry Pressures, Makes Decision to Make Music on Their Own Terms," *Country Now*, November 15, 2023, https://countrynow.com/chapel-hart-bids-farewell-to-industry-pressures-makes-decision-to-make-music-on-their-own-terms/.
10. Marcus K. Dowling, "Blue Collar Roots Thriving: Chapel Hart at Crossroads of Country's Mainstream Growth," *The Tennessean*, February 28, 2024, https://www.tennessean.com/story/entertainment/music/2024/02/28/chapel-hart-country-music-new-genre-trends-sink-trio/71674990007/.
11. Jon Freeman, "Chapel Hart Are Reality TV Darlings Who Write Answer Songs to Dolly and Loretta Hits," *Rolling Stone*, April 21, 2023, https://www.rollingstone.com/music/music-country/chapel-hart-americas-got-talent-you-can-have-him-jolene-1234721347/.

CHAPTER 8

1. Steve Buckingham, personal communication, October 11, 2018.
2. Dolly Parton quoted in Emily Lordi, "Dolly Parton Salutes Rock and Roll," *The New Yorker*, December 3, 2023, https://www.newyorker.com/culture/the-new-yorker-interview/dolly-parton-salutes-rock-and-roll.
3. Pete Keeley, "Dolly Parton on Creating Tunes for 'Dumplin'': 'I Was Playing Off a Lot of My Own Emotions,'" *Billboard*, December 12, 2018, https://www.billboard.com/music/country/dolly-parton-dumplin-interview-8490011/.
4. The Dorian mode is in the melodic lines of the verses—the raised 6th scale degree (C#) is heard in the line (at the italics): "Eleanor Rigby, picks up the rice *in* a *church* where a wedding has been."
5. Dolly Parton quoted in Keeley, "Dolly Parton on Creating Tunes for 'Dumplin'.'"
6. Estelle Tang, "Dolly Parton Never Thinks She's Good Enough," *Elle*, November 28, 2018, https://www.elle.com/culture/music/a25336171/dolly-parton-interview-dumplin-movie-soundtrack/.
7. Hamessley, *Unlikely Angel*, 89–92 and 95–98.

8. Dolly Parton quoted in Carolyn Allen, "The Dolly Parton Interview: Candy Kicker Meets Cinderella," *Picking Up the Tempo: A Country Western Journal* 13 (December/January 1976): 2.
9. Dolly Parton quoted in Tang, "Dolly Parton Never Thinks She's Good Enough."
10. https://twitter.com/dollyparton/status/1063479440548728838.
11. Parton quoted in Keeley, "Dolly Parton on Creating Tunes for 'Dumplin'.'"
12. Robyn Bahr, "'Dolly Parton's Heartstrings': TV Review," *Hollywood Reporter*, November 20, 2019, https://www.hollywoodreporter.com/tv/tv-reviews/dolly-partons-heartstrings-review-1256536/. Reflecting on the episode later, Dolly explained: "They had thought about [the homoerotic reading of the story] when we were doing the 'Jolene' movie when we were writing the script. Someone came up with that basic idea, to say 'wouldn't it be cool if the two women just dumped him . . . both of them dumped him, dumped the guy altogether and went on with their lives as friends?'" Parton quoted in Abumrad and Oliaee, *Dolly Parton's America*, episode 6.
13. Kimberly Williams-Paisley quoted in Meredith Jacobs, "Kimberly Williams-Paisley on the Tension of 'Jolene' in 'Dolly Parton's Heartstrings,'" *TV Insider*, November 21, 2019, https://www.tvinsider.com/834473/kimberly-williams-paisley-dolly-partons-heartstrings-jolene-flash/.
14. Trea Swindle, interview with the author.
15. Dolly wrote this song in 1968 in response to her husband's hurt feelings when he learned that Dolly had had sex before she met him.
16. The lyrics sung in the episode are slightly altered from Dolly's original recording.
17. Leigh H. Edwards, "Dolly Parton's Netflix Reimaging: How Her Twenty-First Century 'Jolene' Revises Country Music's Authenticity Narrative," in *Whose Country Music? Genre, Identity, and Belonging in Twenty-First-Century Music Culture*, Paula J. Bishop and Jada Watson, eds. (Cambridge: Cambridge University Press, 2022), 134.
18. The 2001 film *Women Talking Dirty* plays with a similar scenario and uses "Jolene" as a commentary.

CHAPTER 9

1. Dolly Parton, *Dolly Parton: 50 Years at the Opry*, aired November 26, 2019, on NBC.
2. Parton quoted in Abumrad and Oliaee, *Dolly Parton's America*, episode 6.
3. Parton, *Dolly: My Life and Other Unfinished Business*, 129.
4. Dolly Parton, *Nightline*, "Dolly Parton Unplugged," interviewed by Juju Chang, aired November 26, 2012, on ABC; article and video at Juju Chang and Victoria Thompson, "Dolly Parton on Gay Rumors, New Memoir,"

https://abcnews.go.com/Entertainment/dolly-parton-gay-rumors-losing-drag-queen-alike/story?id=17812138.

5. Parton, *Dolly: My Life and Other Unfinished Business*, 127.
6. Nash, *Dolly: The Biography*, 136; and Eng, *A Satisfied Mind*, 320.
7. Dolly Parton quoted in Toby Thompson, "Dolly Parton Looks Back on Good Old Days When Times Were Bad," *The Village Voice* 21, no. 16 (April 19, 1976): 13.
8. Dolly Parton quoted in Jerry Bailey, "Say Hello to the Real Miss Dolly," *Tennessean Magazine*, October 20, 1974, 5.
9. Sexwale quoted in Abumrad and Oliaee, *Dolly Parton's America*, episode 6.
10. Thompson, "Dolly Parton Looks Back on Good Old Days When Times Were Bad," 13.
11. Parton quoted in Vitale, "Dolly Parton's 'Jolene.' "

INDEX

For the benefit of digital users, indexed terms that span two pages (e.g., 52–53) may, on occasion, appear on only one of those pages.

Figures are indicated by an italic *f* following the page number.